COUSINS

All We Got Is Us!

SELENA
HASKINS

To request permission, contact:
booksbyselena@gmail.com
Paperback ISBN: 979-8-218-37026-8
Published by Calidream Publishing
Edited by Emily Michel
Cover Design: BP Univerx
Book formatting: Karen Perkins Lionheart Publishing
Printed in the USA.

Calidream Publishing
12138 Central Avenue
Suite 869
Mitchellville, MD 20721

BooksbySelena.com
Follow Selena Haskins on social media:
@BooksbySelena

This book is dedicated to the Alston family, especially my cousins.

Time and distance may keep us apart, but we will always be connected at heart.
We were family from the start.
I loved you yesterday, today, and forever.

—Lena

Author's Note:

This book is part one of a two-part series. It's meant to be nostalgic for adult readers who grew up during the 80s and 90s but is intended for young adult readers. My goal is to bring back a moment in time when living on Capitol Hill was about family, community, and togetherness. Through good times and bad times, our family always had each other, and sometimes our friends had our back too. I hope you enjoy reading this story as much as I enjoyed writing it. Stay tuned for part two when the characters become adults, and it will be intended for adult readers.

-Selena Haskins

PART I

THE WALKER COUSINS

CHAPTER 1
SILENT SUMMER
1986

LESLIE WALKER

My mother was mute. She wasn't born that way. She was raped. My grandmother, Beulah May Walker, told me Mama stopped talking shortly after that. She said Mama's mind went someplace else and never came back. As for my father, who I asked about when I was five, Grandma had told me his name was Percy Knight. She said Percy was a monster but assured me he was never coming back.

I found comfort in knowing that Grandma would always protect me, but she couldn't stop the mean girls at school who had teased me for being fat and said Mama was a spook. Whenever Mama would look out her bedroom window as the children walked to and from school, they would point and laugh and call Mama a "Window Witch." By the time I was seven, I had learned how to braid Mama's wild hair like I had done with my dolls. I had hoped this would stop the children from teasing her, but they continued since there wasn't anything I could do to stop her ghostly stare.

"Don't you worry about those children at school. Your mother's eyes are a window to her soul, and you will be able to tell how she feels," Grandma would say.

Over the years, I learned that when Mama was happy, her eyes would light up, and when she was sad, they appeared cloudy and distant. By the time I was twelve, Grandma taught me how to sew and cook for Mama.

Although Mama could do some things on her own, we never knew when her mind would travel someplace else, especially when dealing with appliances. She had left a pot of food on the stove, and it burned, and another time she had placed her curling iron in the kitchen sink. Thankfully, there wasn't any dishwater in the sink.

We always had to stay alert when it came to Mama, even though she expressed herself in an unusual way. Yesterday, she was clapping her hands and smiling for no apparent reason. I called Grandma upstairs to her room. I had never seen Mama behave that way.

"What is it, Irene? You can tell us." Grandma had stroked Mama's hand. I hoped Mama would finally talk. Instead, we watched in disappointment as her eyes turned into a shadow of teary-eyed gloom and she retreated to her bed. Curiously, I looked out her bedroom window to see what she may have been excited about, and all I saw were a group of pigeons eating the old bread that Grandma had tossed out to them. Maybe whatever Mama saw was in her mind. I have a shell for a mother, and I can't seem to peel off the layers of her pain to see if she has a heart inside that can love me just a little bit.

"Leslie!" Grandma called for me from downstairs. I finished writing the last sentence in my diary and hurried out of my room.

"Yes ma'am?" I leaned over the banister in the hallway.

"Your Aunt Diane just pulled up and tooted the horn three times for you," Grandma said, standing at the bottom of the steps in her flowery housedress and fuzzy slippers.

"Okay, I'm coming..." I rushed back to my room and grabbed my suitcase. I was excited to go stay the weekend at Aunt Diane's house. She and her daughter Raven held a sleepover every year for all my cousins when school let out for the summer. They live in Clinton, Maryland, a twenty-minute ride from my house on Capitol Hill in DC.

"That was the fastest I have ever seen you move. Keep it up and you may lose a few pounds," Grandma chuckled as I met her at the bottom of the stairs.

I just turned fifteen and weighed 150 pounds during my last doctor's visit. He said I needed to go on a diet. Grandma's idea of dieting was one piece of fried chicken and tossing a lemon in my Kool-Aid. And my idea of dieting was no diet at all. I ate certain foods according to how I was feeling. If I was sad, I found comfort in a bowl of Rocky Road ice cream. If I was bored, I ate slices of Al's pizza. When I was nervous, I'd use my allowance and buy a bag full of five-cent candy from Ms. Clark's. I knew I needed to work on my weight, but since it was summer I would do it later.

"See you on Sunday, Grandma." I leaned down slightly to hug her. She was a little shorter than me, top-heavy, and had a cheeky smile.

"Bye sugar," Grandma walked me to the door and watched as I made my way across the street to Aunt Diane's Audi 5000.

"Are you planning to move in or something?" Aunt Diane poked her head out the window.

"No ma'am, I didn't want to forget anything," I said. She popped open the trunk, and I tossed my suitcase inside, then hopped into the back seat.

"Hey Raven," I said to my cousin, who was sitting in the front passenger seat.

Raven turned around and beamed a jovial smile as she replied, "Hey Cuz."

I noticed she had the new asymmetric hairdo all the girls were wearing these days. It was cute, but it made Raven look sixteen instead of thirteen.

"What took you so long? I blew the horn three times," Aunt Diane complained as she drove off.

"Sorry, I didn't hear it. I was writing in my diary, and you know my room is toward the back."

"I bet I know who you were writing about," Raven chortled. She was a twin version of her mother with the same honey-colored eyes, long dark hair, and skin the color of brown sugar. There were no physical traces of her father

3

Raymond, whom the family often called a "light-skinned pretty boy" with glasses.

"How do you know?" I asked, nervously.

"You left it open the last time I was over," she said. "I know you had a crush on a guy named Alex. You also said you hoped he would join you this coming school year at Eastern when you start ninth grade."

I huffed and crossed my arms, shaking my head in disbelief.

"Raven, you shouldn't have done that." Aunt Diane took the words right out of my mouth. I loved Raven like a younger sister, but I was upset that she read my diary. She couldn't hold water if you sealed her lips with superglue.

"Leslie, maybe you shouldn't tell *everything* in your diary and keep some things to yourself," Aunt Diane advised. I could tell her lawyer radar was sounding off. She was a personal injury attorney who helped her clients sue for compensation. Grandma said she was trying to make partner, whatever that means.

"How is your mom doing these days?" Aunt Diane skipped the subject. I hated how she asked about Mama as if she lived in a faraway place.

"Maybe you should stop by her room when you drop me off on Sunday."

"If Irene's mood is right, I will," she said. "Too bad the doctors could never find the right medicine for her."

"Doctors?"

"Yes, the doctors at St. Elizabeth Hospital."

"Wait, I never knew Mama was at St. Elizabeth."

"Forget I mentioned it." Diane waved off the thought. "Just know that your mother wasn't always the way she is now."

"Then, how was she?"

"She was smart, just like you. Your grandparents doted on her all the time. She could do no wrong. She also loved dancing, and we would party all the time at Breeze Nightclub or the Fox Trap where the elite folks hung out at."

4

"I can't imagine Mama dancing."

"Big sis could cut a rug at the discos in those days, but then...that incident happened and...well never mind. What do you guys want for dinner?" She dropped the subject as she pulled into the Safeway parking lot.

"The usual," Raven and I said in unison.

"The usual? As in the ingredients to make chili cheese hot dogs?"

"Yes," Raven answered. "And don't forget our cookies 'n cream ice cream for dessert."

"We have some in the freezer at home already," Aunt Diane replied, grabbing her Fendi purse as she stepped out of the car one high heel at a time.

"And Little Debbie cakes, please." I leaned my head out the window.

"As long as you promise not to eat them all this time."

"I won't."

I craned my neck to look out the rear window and watched Aunt Diane head into the store. A group of older men who used their cars as taxis to offer customers rides were standing outside. They whistled as Aunt Diane walked by in her short miniskirt outfit. Her long curls bounced off her shoulders like a Dark & Lovely commercial. Aunt Diane was beautiful, and I wished I had a body like hers.

"Hey Leslie," Raven called for my attention. I turned around from the rear window. "Look who I got." She held up New Edition's "All for Love" cassette tape.

"Wow! When did you get that?"

"It came in the mail yesterday. I ordered it from Columbia House for only a penny." She popped the tape in the deck.

"No way!"

"I did. All I had to do was fill out the form in the back of *Right On* magazine, and they sent me twelve tapes for only a penny."

"That's bumpin! I'm going to order some tapes too," I said, snapping my fingers as the melody to the song "Count

Me Out" spewed through the speakers. Raven and I started singing all the lyrics by heart and even smacked our lips to make the kiss sound at the end of the song.

Music always cheered me up and made me forget all that was wrong with the world, especially all that was wrong with Mama.

"Ralph is so cute, he's my favorite New Edition member." Raven admired his picture inside the cassette case.

"I like Bobby Brown. He has a nice smile, and he can dance."

"Bobby is cute, but neither he nor Ralph can top Mitch."

"Mitch? There's no band member named Mitch with New Edition."

"I'm talking about Mitchell Larson who lives across the street from you and Grandma, silly." Raven said, as she ejected the tape, then turned the radio dial. Candy Shannon's beautiful voice came through the speakers as she announced that we were listening to 100.3 WDJY.

"Besides, Mitch and I are getting married. See." Raven held up a piece of paper where she drew a square for the game MASH. The goal was to determine your dwelling place, number of kids, cars, and who you would end up marrying based on the count from your lucky number.

"Wait a minute, you listed Mitch four times as an option for a husband. That's not how the game works."

Raven giggled. "I know. I was trying to increase my chances."

"But Mitch is seventeen. You're only thirteen."

"At least I know how to French kiss like teenagers do."

"Who are you kissing? A preppy scholar from your private school?" I asked, crossing my arms.

"Yep, and he's cute like Kirk Cameron on *Growing Pains*."

"You'd better hope your mother won't find out."

"She's not tripping. You're just jealous because Grandma won't let you have a boyfriend. You'll probably be a hundred years old before she lets you date. By then, your booty will blow dust."

"Shut up!" I plucked the side of her neck.

She winced in pain. "Ow, don't do that again."

Aunt Diane came back to the car with food in the cart. She unloaded the groceries into the trunk and then stepped into the car. Her gaze ping-ponged between me and Raven.

"Why are you two so quiet all of a sudden?" Aunt Diane asked.

"Leslie and I were talking about boys and French kissing."

"Oh my gosh, why would you tell your mother that?" I smacked my hand to my forehead.

"It's not a big deal. Mom and I talk about boys and sex all the time."

"Your stomach looks a little bigger since our last visit. Are you pregnant?" Aunt Diane glared at me from the rearview mirror before backing out of the parking lot.

"What? No way!"

"That's good to know. Well, hopefully you can wear the outfits I just bought you from Hecht's. You're still a size fourteen, right?"

"Yes ma'am." I hoped my protruding belly wouldn't suddenly pop the button off my shorts.

"Good, but I will say we still need to do something about that scary curl on your head."

"You mean my Jheri Curl?"

"No sweetie, Jheri done left a long time ago, it's scary how it looks right about now."

Raven burst out laughing.

"Don't laugh, Raven. We're going to take Leslie to Tish's Crimps and Cuts tomorrow morning." Aunt Diane glared at me. "I may get Serena to do your nails too while we're there. You're starting high school and it's time you look more fashionable."

I crossed my arms and glared out the window. Going to Tish's beauty salon wouldn't be so bad. I could use a new hairstyle. I always trusted Aunt Diane and Raven's taste when it came to style and fashion. They had every name brand of jeans from Jordache to Guess, and all the shoes, including Agnes and Ryder boots that they wore during the winter. They liked to shop at high-end stores like Hetch's, Lord & Taylor, and Talbots. Grandma always took me to McBride's or Morton's.

"Are we going to pick up Donovan now?" I asked.

"Yes, and afterward, we will scoop up Champ and Boogie since they're en route to my house."

"Good," I said with a smirk. I knew their conversations would break the monotony of all this bourgeois girly talk.

CHAPTER 2
SUMMERTIME BLUES

DONOVAN "LUCCI" WALKER, JR.

As I cleaned the rims of my great-cousin Turk's gold-colored Nissan 300ZX, I bobbed my head to Rare Essence's song "Back Up Against the Wall." The song echoed a funky mix of percussions, congas, and drums from the tape deck inside the car. DC was known for its go-go bands, from Chuck Brown, Air Raid, Little Benny, Junk Yard, and of course, Rare Essence. Everyone on the block of Arthur Cappers housing projects was jamming to "Back Up Against the Wall" as it played so loud it echoed throughout the block.

"You missed a spot." Turk pointed out. I wiped the waxy smear until it was shining smoothly. Turk walked around the car to examine it further. When he smiled, I knew I finally had his approval. Turk's car was the fifth car I had washed today, and I was tired as a mug, but I had made fifty dollars so far.

"Good job, shorty." Turk praised my work and flipped through the spool of large bills, but when he got to the tens and fives, he handed me a ten-dollar bill.

"Did you make all that money at Erol's video store?" I asked, just to see if he would tell me the truth. I knew he was a drug dealer.

"Something like that," Turk answered, leaning his tall penny-colored frame against the car. I could not take my eyes off the beautiful gold herringbone chain glistening around his neck. It complemented his MCM white and black Dapper Dan short set. Turk was always fly. He had showed me pictures from his trip to the Bahamas, where he had celebrated his thirtieth birthday like he was a movie star.

"How can I make money like you?" I poked out my chest, feeling proud to be thirteen. I tried to flex my muscles like I was ready to stomp with the big boys.

Turk twirled a toothpick in his mouth. "Do you really want to know how I make money?"

"Heck yeah!"

"I'll tell you, but first, there's something I need to know."

I looked up at him and jerked my head back. "What?"

"A little birdie told me you been breaking into people's houses again and stealing food out their refrigerators. Is that true?"

I opened my mouth to speak, then snapped it shut to think about my answer before I blurted out the first thing that came to my mind. I didn't want Turk to think less of me. He already knew about my thirty-day stint in juvie. I had gotten arrested for stealing a box of half-smokes out of Murry's steakhouse on 8th Street. I tried to sell the half-smokes, hoping to buy a pair of New Balance 1300s from Snyders, but the owner of the store had caught me by Eastern Market and called Five-o.

"Answer my question," Turk insisted, removing his EK glasses and staring at me with his dark piercing eyes.

"All I can say is, I'm trying to buy one of those Adidas sweatsuits."

Turk's eyes traced over me, and when his pupils landed on my feet, his lips turned up in a slight grin. I could tell he was trying not to laugh at my dusty, holey sneakers. They were so old that the laces had popped when I had tried to tie them.

"I like how you dodged that question, shorty. You better stay out of people's houses before you get smoked."

"Give me some more money, then."

"Here." Turk peeled off another ten-dollar bill.

"Man, this will buy me some Oodles of Noodles and a

case of Little Hug juices, but this ain't enough to save for a sweatsuit unless you buy it for me."

"You're pushing your luck, shorty." Turk handed me a twenty. "I never paid forty dollars for a car wash with old rags."

"Sure you right," I said, in my best Chuck Brown impression as I leaned down and tucked the money in my sock like I'd seen Turk do. "You got all that money and you're complaining."

Turk's face twisted as he tried not to laugh. He knew I was right. "You're too smart for your own good, you little beady-headed rascal."

"DON-O-VAN!"

I looked over my shoulder. It was my mother calling me from the front porch. Her hair was matted to her scalp, eyes dark like a raccoon, and her knees were ashy like she had been crawling in flour.

"Your Aunt Diane should be here in a minute, so come and pack your drawers."

"Theresa, don't put that man's business in the streets like that."

"He ain't a man. He's just a boy," she said, walking over to us barefoot as she scratched her polka-dot arms. "You got a little something for me?"

"You know not to ask me that." Turk shot Mom a mean look. She clucked her teeth like a child, turned around, and walked back into the house.

"I need to jet, little cuz." Turk gave me a fist pound. "From now on, I'm calling you Lucci."

I puckered my brow. "Lucci?"

"Yeah, Lucci. It means money. You like making money, and you seem to be doing anything to get it. Besides, every time I call you Donovan, I think about your father, and he was a sucker for doing somebody else's time."

"Hey man, my daddy ain't no sucker."

"If I say he is, then he is."

"Well, do they call you Turk 'cuz that's short for turkey?"

"Watch it!" Turk warned with a pointy finger. "You stay out of trouble before they throw you in a real jail with your old man."

"Yeah, whatever...stingy mug," I mumbled.

"What did you say?"

"Nothing." I whistled and walked away, going inside the house.

I immediately smelled the aroma of bacon and eggs mixed with cigarette smoke. My mother's boyfriend Earl was sitting on the couch wearing a dingy looking white tank top, while the *Price is Right* played on the TV. His hands were the size of two football fields, so I knew he and Mom had been shooting up again. Earl used to be Mom's trick, you know, a guy she used for money to get her drug fix. Somehow, Earl got a taste of what my mother was doing and got hooked on that junk, too. I'd seen the syringes in the bathroom a few times.

I walked by Earl and accidentally knocked over the picture of Aunt Gloria sitting on the table. She was Turk's mom. She died before I was born.

"Pick it up!" Earl snarled at me. I moved extremely slow on purpose, like I needed oil in my knees like the Tin Man from the *Wizard of Oz*. I wanted to make him angry. He was a fat slob who didn't deserve to be with my mother.

I picked up the picture and held it in my hand, staring at a stoic-faced Aunt Gloria. I hadn't noticed how serious she looked until now. She was sitting on the front steps of her house wearing a long fur coat. She was surrounded by women in short skirts and high heels. They wore lots of makeup on their faces, including my mother, who was standing behind her. I recalled the story my mother told me about moving from New York to DC with Aunt Gloria and Turk. She didn't get along with her mother and came to DC when she was fifteen. When Aunt Gloria died, my mom and Turk were homeless. A DC social worker put Mom and Turk in foster care, but they kept running away. Eventually, Mom ended up having me at sixteen. She moved into the

Second Chance homes on East Capitol Street until she turned eighteen. Afterward, she applied for public housing and moved us here to Arthur Cappers, called "Capers" by the folks who live here.

Turk grew up living pillow-to-post, but eventually he started making money to survive. I learned all this partially from Mom and partially from my dad when he would call collect. Sometimes I wondered if I would end up like them.

"I said put the picture down!" Earl projected his voice louder. I gingerly kissed the picture and set it back down on the coffee table.

"Sorry, Aunt Glo," I said, then casually walked into the kitchen. I tried to irritate Earl every chance I got hoping he would stop coming around, but he was like a pesky fly that never gave up.

"Is that for me?" I asked, practically drooling at the breakfast plate Mom held in her hand. The cereal I had eaten earlier with water was long gone. It was the middle of the day, but Mom and Earl always hung out until the wee hours of morning and slept in late.

"No, this plate is for Earl," she chided, as a cigarette bounced from the corner of her mouth with each word she spoke. She searched the kitchen, looking for silverware, and tried to switch her bony hips from side-to-side.

"Close that dang refrigerator!" Mom shouted.

I slammed the door shut. The only thing left inside the fridge anyway was a pack of stale-looking bologna and a dried-up block of cheese. Earl had eaten up all our food.

I reached up and grabbed a small box of sweet popcorn off the top of the refrigerator. The flap had been left opened, and when I tilted the box to my hungry mouth, a huge cockroach with a twitching antenna crawled out.

"EWWW!" I jumped and the box fell on the floor.

"Kill it!" Mom shouted, as the roach sprinted behind the refrigerator.

"It's too late, it's gone now." I shook my head. I gave up on my search for food and went upstairs to pack the few pieces of clothes I had.

In my room, I emptied my money from washing cars into an empty Mello Yello soda bottle that I had stashed in the back of my closet. I pulled out a pair of underwear from a broken dresser drawer and tossed it in a plastic People's Drug Store bag. I kept trying to ignore my stomach howling like a wolf was inside of me, but I was so hungry. At least at the juvie and school, I got regular meals twice a day. I had tried to flunk my tests so I could end up in summer school just so I could have a meal. Despite trying to answer the test questions like I was stupid, I still passed. Lucky for me, I will still be going to Jefferson Junior High for seventh grade in September.

I went back downstairs and flopped down on the sunken loveseat across from Earl and my mom. I watched Earl cram food into his mouth like a hog and then guzzle down a can of beer. He was armpit funky, and his belly rested on his thighs. When Mom leaned to the side to kiss Earl's chubby, bearded cheek, I could feel the bitterness in the back of my throat. She never kissed or hugged me like that, but she was doting on this stank fatso.

"Why are you staring at me, boy?" Earl sneered. He had a head full of gray hair with a bald spot in the middle. He also wore a wedding band. If I had to guess, I would say he was in his early 60s and married. He knew better than to be messing with my mother, who was only twenty-nine.

"Nothing," I murmured, puffing my cheeks. *And I do mean nothing.*

"Theresa, you need to handle that boy."

"Oh, leave him alone. He will be out of our hair in a minute."

"I don't like the way he looks at me," Earl grumbled.

"He looks at every man who comes in here in that way."

Earl narrowed his eyes at her. "What do you mean by *every man* that comes in here?"

Mom coyly crossed one skinny leg over the other and said, "Aw Boo, don't get jealous."

Suddenly, Earl grabbed Mom by the throat. "Winch, don't play with me like that!"

My body jolted from the loveseat. "Get your hands off my mother, fool."

"Earl...let me go...pleeease," Mom squealed.

"I said, get your hands off her!" I charged at Earl and punched him with my fists as hard as I could. With all that blubber around his spine, he didn't even budge.

Earl released Mom's skinny neck and spun around so quickly that I didn't see his mitten-sized hand coming for my face. He knocked me to the floor and stood over me like he was about to finish me off.

"That's enough," Mom hissed, gasping for air. "Donovan's Aunt Diane just pulled up outside. She's a lawyer with connections and her brother is a cop."

"Next time, it's me and you, boy. And I don't care who your other family is," Earl threatened with a pointy finger and nostrils flared like a bull.

My knees buckled as I rose from the floor. I felt dazed by Earl's punch and staggered over to the sofa to grab my bag. I tried to shake it off, but I was in pain as I made my way to the door.

"Hold up." Mom jumped in front of me. "Don't snitch about what just happened in here, do you hear me, boy?"

She poked my chest with her finger. I could feel the anger swelling in the pit of my stomach. Reluctantly, I nodded my head yes, but I was tired of Earl beating on me all the time.

"Go on to the car." She nudged her head.

I hurried to Aunt Diane's car, jumped in, and slammed the door so hard the windows rattled.

"Boy, don't be slamming my door like you lost your good sense!" Aunt Diane turned around sharply. When she saw my swollen cheek, her pupils dilated with concern.

"What happened to you?" she asked.

"Nothing," I mumbled, sucking in my cheeks tightly. I could hear Mom's words, *don't snitch.*

"Are you sure you're, okay?" Leslie asked. She was sitting next to me. I sucked my teeth and rolled my eyes at her.

"Did your mother hit you?" Aunt Diane asked but didn't wait for me to answer before she hopped out of the car and marched to my front door. Her voice erupted at Earl and my mom, who stood in the doorway.

"What did y'all do to my nephew?" Aunt Diane yelled. From there, an argument ensued, with Aunt Diane doing most of the yelling. Everyone on the block and everything in motion stopped moving to see what was going on at my house. For a split second, Earl looked a little scared. The argument ended with Aunt Diane telling Earl, "If you lay another hand on my nephew, I promise you won't see the light of day ever again. And I will make sure my colleagues put you in the same prison cell with Donovan's father."

As Aunt Diane climbed back into the car, I could tell by the fierce look in her eyes that she meant business. She helped my father find a new criminal defense attorney to try to appeal his case, so she knew lots of folks in the legal field.

"Earl said he hit you because you stole money from his wallet, but I don't care what you did, he had no business bruising your face like that. You're not a man. You're a child."

"I never took nothing from Earl," I protested, saying to myself, *not this time.*

"I could tell he was lying by the way his eyes kept jerking," she declared. "And another thing, I warned your mother if she doesn't go to rehab, I'm calling child protective services on her."

"But if you do that, he will end up adopted like Mitch," Raven interjected from the front seat.

"Well, something has to be done," Aunt Diane asserted. "Donovan can't stay in that environment if his mother doesn't get help soon."

"Call me Lucci."

"Excuse me?" Aunt Diane glared at me briefly from the rearview mirror.

"Lucci, it means money," I said, holding my aching jaw with one hand like I had a toothache.

"Whatever, boy. I'm stopping at this corner store and get you some ice for your face." Aunt Diane pulled over.

Leslie turned to me and said, "You know we always have your back, right?" She rested her hand on top of mine. I felt kind of bad for being mean to her. She was like my big sister. But I did not want anyone to feel sorry for me.

"Don't sweat it. I'm not worried about Earl, but if he hits me like that again, he's going to regret it. I promise you that."

"God said that vengeance is his," Leslie stated.

"Well then, I pray God grants me the same power he gave David when he killed that giant with a rock."

"You're a trip, Lucci."

"Nope, I'm a journey with no luggage."

CHAPTER 3
CASH FUN

NOLAN "BOOGIE" WALKER

"Funky Beat" by Whodini was playing on 93-WKYS from the small radio in our kitchen window while I was cornrowing Mom's hair. Champ and Dad were in the living room talking about basketball *again*. Dad liked the Celtics and Champ was a Lakers fan. The two of them were debating who was the greatest between Bird and Magic. If I were part of the debate, I would choose Magic for his smile. Bird always looked like he didn't have any emotions, although he had a nice jump shot.

"Don't make the cornrows too skinny, they will be hard to take out," Mom said to me, checking the style before the hand mirror.

"As you wish." I smiled into the mirror in her hand, and she smiled back before placing it back on her lap.

I loved braiding Mom's long reddish-brown hair. She and Champ looked just alike. He had a head full of curly reddish-brown hair, and all the girls loved to run their fingers through it. I look more like my father. We both have medium bronze skin, big round marble-shaped eyes, and pointy ears. The only difference between Dad and me is that I didn't inherit the Walker men's height. I'm short. Mom used to call me "Chipmunk." She said I looked like one of those cute Monchhichi dolls. I'm twelve now. Mom doesn't call me Chipmunk anymore. She calls me "Boogie" because I love to dance.

My dad said a man shouldn't do a woman's hair, but I learned how to braid from playing with Barbie dolls with

Raven when we were kids. I love the feeling of stringy hair between my fingers. Sometimes Grandma lets me style her hair in crochet curls like Curly Sue for church. I learned by watching Leslie when she'd style her mother's hair. Too bad my hair isn't long enough to curl or else I'd wear it like Prince.

A loud horn from outside caught our attention.

"That's probably your Aunt Diane," Mom said, just as I had finished the last braid on her head. It was summer, and Mom liked to wear her hair in braids so her scalp could breathe the warm air.

"I'll go grab me and Champ's night bags," I said, setting the comb down on the kitchen table. I dashed upstairs to retrieve our bags from our shared room, slung both duffel bags over my shoulders and carried them downstairs.

"Oh, thanks, Shrimp." Champ took his bag from me. "I was just about to go upstairs to get this." Champ always called me shrimp because I was small for my age. People often think I'm nine or ten.

"I'm surprised you could carry both of those heavy bags," Dad observed.

"I got muscles, that's why." I flexed my biceps.

Dad chuckled. "Not like Champ, you don't. You're as skinny as a beanpole."

"Oh Henry, don't discourage your son," Mom said as we all walked to the door.

"Wait," Champ stopped. "I forgot to pack my ball."

He ran upstairs to our room. You would've thought he had forgotten something important like house keys, a wallet, or medication, but nope. Champ never went anywhere without Spalding.

"Make it quick son, you know your Aunt Diane is impatient," Dad reminded him, just as we heard her tooting the horn again.

It was Dad who nicknamed my big brother, Henry Walker Jr., "Champ" because he had won basketball championships every school year since he started playing at seven years old. He is a seventeen-year-old basketball sensation now. I'm not just saying that because he is my brother. The trophies on the mantel above our fireplace speak for themselves.

Dad opened the door, and Donovan looked like he was just about to ring the doorbell.

"Aunt Diane said are y'all ready?" Donovan asked.

"Well, hello to you too, Donovan." Dad reminded him of his manners.

"Hi Uncle Henry and Aunt Naomi," Donovan said with a half-smile. "By the way, you guys can call me Lucci now."

"Why should we call you Lucci? What's that mean?" I propped one hand on my hip.

"It means money. I'm gonna make a lot of it one day."

"Sure you right!" Champ laughed.

"What happened to your face?" I asked.

"I got in a fight."

"Sheesh, I hope you won." Dad narrowed his eyes at the purplish bruise on the side of Lucci's face.

"You better be careful out there, nephew." Mom's eyebrows wrinkled with concern.

"You boys got some spending money?" Dad's voice boomed like Barry White. His big hands reached into his pocket and retrieved his wallet.

"No, but I'll take some." I flipped my wrist. Dad gave me the side eye and a smirk.

"Here, and don't spend it all in one place," Dad planted a ten-dollar bill in my hand and gave another ten to Champ.

"Thanks, Dad." Champ rushed out the door, brushing past Lucci. He jumped into the backseat of Aunt Diane's car. She had parked next to Dad's DC Police patrol car. He usually drove it home when he was going to have a long shift over the weekend. Sometimes Dad lets Champ and me ride with him and play the sirens. We always get a kick out of watching cars move to the side of the road, thinking they were going to get a ticket.

As I was putting the ten dollars in my pocket, I caught

Lucci staring. He dropped his eyes to the ground, turned around, and whistled as he walked to Aunt Diane's car. The dingy shorts he wore looked like he cut them from an old pair of jeans, and the soles of his shoes were held together with bubblegum. He was not only a fashion disaster, but he looked like he'd been sleeping in the streets or something. Donovan never had the best of things, but he looked like he was getting worse.

"Wait Cuz, here, you can have my money." I handed him my ten-dollar bill. He looked like he needed it more.

"No need for that, Nolan." Dad thumbed through the bills in his wallet. "Come here, Donovan, I mean, Lucci, or whatever you want to be called. I can't leave you hanging. Look at you, just growing like a weed. You look like you could use a few extra bucks, though." Dad handed Lucci a twenty-dollar bill.

"Wow, thanks, Uncle Henry!" Lucci bent down and put the money in his dingy sock.

"You're welcome. Have you talked to your father lately?"

"No, our phone got cut off." Lucci's eyelids drooped as if he felt embarrassed.

"That's a shame." Dad shook his head. "Be sure and write him a letter. You can buy stamps with the money I gave you, okay?"

Lucci nodded. "Alright."

"Lucci, you're almost as tall as Champ," Mom observed. "I was just about to wash some of his old clothes before donating them to charity, but I'd rather give them to family."

"You got any Guess jeans or some AJs, so I can look bumpin?"

"Sure do, and a few Le Coq Sportif sweatsuits that you may like. I'll have them for you on Sunday after your sleepover."

"Cool."

"Are you playing any ball these days, Lucci?" Dad asked.

"Sometimes I play ball at Randall Recreation Center."

"Keep playing and you may be as good as Champ one day. Sports run in the Walker family, you know," Dad said, proudly. "Your father and I played basketball for Eastern, and your aunts played softball during the summer for a team called Blue Jays."

"I think I saw old trophies at Grandma's house," Lucci recalled.

Aunt Diane stuck her head out the window and shouted, "Is this a family reunion? Let's go already."

"Well, you boys had better get going." Mom hugged us both.

I tried to stop staring at Lucci's cheek, but I couldn't help it. I reached out and touched it with my hand. "I hope you got them back for hitting you like this."

Lucci whimpered. "Ow, don't touch it!"

"Nolan, leave him alone and hurry along, will ya?" Dad shooed me with his hand. He never called me "Boogie" like the rest of the family. I hated that he named me Nolan after his former police partner who was killed in the line of duty.

Lucci and I quickly hopped in the car.

"Boogie, they're playing you and Lucci's song," Raven announced from the front seat. Her hair looked fly. I loved the asymmetric style. She turned the volume up to Run DMC rapping "My Adidas."

"Ready to rap the song, Lucci?" I asked.

"Let's get it, Cuz!" Lucci was hyped up. He and I started rapping the whole song, and Champ and Leslie did the human beatbox with their lips. I loved being with my cousins. We were going to have cash fun!

CHAPTER 4
HOT FUN IN THE SUMMERTIME

RAVEN WALKER-BROOKS

My mother was a germaphobe. We always had to remove our shoes at the door. She didn't want us messing up the white wall-to-wall carpet.

"Raven, I'm going to start dinner. Remind your cousins where the linens are," Mom instructed as she headed toward the kitchen.

"Right this way, my lovely cousins," I said in a gingerly tone, the way I had seen Kimberly do on *Diff'rent Strokes* TV show. They followed me up the spiral staircase, where I handed them fresh towels and washcloths from the hallway linen closet.

"You know the routine, guys. Ladies first and we go one at a time." I propped my hand on my hip in a gesture I'd always seen my mother and grandmother do.

By the time we finished our showers, Mom had dinner ready. We sat around the long cherrywood dining room table wearing our pajamas as we ate chili dogs and french fries. Lucci was eating his hot dogs so fast that he barely chewed them up good before packing his mouth with another one. He was also the only cousin *without* his own pajamas. I had loaned him a pair of my old gym shorts and a T-shirt with *The Flintstones* on it.

"Dang boy, you act like you never ate before," I teased Lucci.

"You're barely eating at all," Lucci snapped back, his voice muffled since his mouth was full of food.

I tilted up my chin. "I'm watching my figure."

"What figure?" Champ smirked. "You bony little winch."

Everyone laughed. I knew not to take Champ seriously. He was always joaning on me.

After we ate dinner, we went into the living room to watch *Soul Train*. I grabbed the remote to turn the volume up on the floor model color TV that my mom had just bought. The singing group Cameo was performing their latest hit, "Word Up." When the Soul Train dancers started doing the Soul Train line, we knew it was time for us to do the same. It was part of our usual dance contest to see who had the best moves.

Standing in his matching blue pajama set, Boogie started doing "The Prep," when you rock your shoulders from left to right with your hands in the air like you're juggling balls. Leslie and I danced along with Boogie.

"It's you guys' turn now." Leslie urged Lucci and Champ to get off the sofa. Champ joined in and started pop-locking and swerving his long arms like the motion of big waves. He was taller than all of us, including Leslie who was two years younger than him. Leslie was going to be a freshman at Eastern, and Champ was going to be a junior at DeMatha Catholic High. He'd been there since freshman year on a basketball scholarship.

"I can do that." Boogie stepped forward, and he did the wave, moving his entire body like a slinky.

"Aw shucks, get it, Boogie!" Mom cheered, stepping into the living room to peep at what we were doing. I loved Mom, but she was nosy like Grandma sometimes.

"Watch this, Aunt Diane." Champ stepped in front of Boogie and started breakdancing on the floor. He put his long arms between his legs and hopped around like a cricket while Boogie did the centipede across the floor. When the song concluded, Champ stood up and crossed his arms in a B-boy stance.

"Who won? I bet I won," Champ boasted.

"Boogie won!" We all said in unison, including Mom.

"What prize did Boogie win?" Champ was anxious to know.

"Nothing. He just won," I shrugged.

"Boooo, that sucks!" Champ gestured a thumbs down.

"The prize was beating you, freckle face," Boogie teased, and the two of them ended up wrestling on the floor.

"One...two..." Lucci counted down like he was the referee of their wrestling match, slapping his hand against the floor. "Three!"

"I won!" Champ thrusted his arms in the air.

"Satisfied now?" Boogie got upset and pouted.

"Aw, Shrimp, don't be mad." Champ rubbed the top of Boogie's thick, curly hair.

"Leave me alone! Don't touch me!" Boogie sulked.

"Anyone feel like a *friendly* game of Monopoly?" Leslie grabbed the box off the oval-shaped glass table. Mom and I had stacked boxes of board games in preparation for the sleepover. We bought them from Toys "R" Us.

"Give me the dice. I'm going first." Champ stretched out his hand to Leslie.

"No, let the youngest one start first." Leslie gently placed the dice in Boogie's hand. And just like that, Boogie had forgotten about losing to his brother in wrestling.

"I'm the banker." Lucci started setting up the colorful money in each plastic slot as we sat in a circle on the living room floor.

"But I want to be the banker." Champ lightly shoved Lucci, and Lucci elbowed him back.

"Cut it out, Champ!" Leslie shouted. "Lucci is the banker, and he controls the properties, too."

Champ gritted his teeth. "Fine, but can I at least be the car, dang?"

"No." I snatched the car out of the box. "I'm the car."

"Girls can't be the car."

"Why not? My dad drives a Porsche like this."

"Exactly, your *dad* does, not your mom, because she's a woman."

"Don't be a chauvinist, Champ," Leslie stated.

"Oh alright," Champ sighed. "I guess I'll take the shoe and imagine they're Air Jordan."

Champ ended up being the winner of the Monopoly game, but it was close between him and Lucci. I honestly think Lucci was just tired since he started dozing off.

"Donovan, your dad is on the phone for you." Mom walked into the living room with the cordless phone in her hand.

"I told you to call me Lucci."

"Whatever, boy. Come and grab this phone."

Lucci took the phone, and for a minute it seemed like his dad did most of the talking because Lucci was just holding the phone to his ear. Eventually, I overheard Lucci telling his father that his mother's boyfriend Earl had punched him in the face for standing up for his mother. We were playing a game of Trouble, but I listened to their conversation on the sneak tip. Uncle Donovan got loud. He sounded mad that Earl hit his son. I was mad too. I didn't want Lucci to end up in CPS, but like Mom said, something had to change. Too bad his father wasn't here to help. I heard so many family rumors about him killing someone or taking the blame for someone else who did. I wasn't sure what to believe and my mom always got mad whenever I asked.

The next day, we took Leslie to Tish, who styled Leslie's hair in the popular 80s snatch-back hairdo. The boys got their haircut at Steve and Dink's barbershop next door. Afterward, we took Lucci shopping, and Mom bought him the Adidas sweatsuit he wanted.

After all the grooming and shopping, Mom took us to Crystal's Skating Rink in Hillcrest Heights, Maryland, about ten minutes from our house.

"Leslie, keep an eye on everyone," Mom reminded her. Although Leslie wasn't the oldest among us, she was the responsible one.

"Yes ma'am."

"Please stop calling me 'ma'am' like I'm old. I'm only thirty-six."

"But Grandma said to address my elders as ma'am or sir. She also said—"

"I don't care what else my mother told you. It's 1986 not 1968."

We all laughed. Leslie could be old-fashioned with the things she said and did at times.

"I will pick you guys up at six, so keep an eye on the time," Mom said, then she left.

"Party time. Let's get it!" Champ rushed into the rink.

A group of girls who were leaning on the rink border wall were gawking at Champ like he was a celebrity. Champ happened to glance over his shoulder, and when he spotted the girls looking at him, he winked. The girls blushed and giggled as he skated by them.

"He's so cute," I overheard them say, as I skated out onto the rink to join him.

Girls always loved Champ. When we had gone to Kings Dominion amusement park for our family reunion, there were a bunch of girls who had followed Champ around. They got on every ride that he rode and played every game he played. I think Champ loved Spalding more than any girl who blushed at him.

We all tried to keep up with Champ in the skating rink. I had sweat out my curls, and my bangs were flopping over my eyes. I needed to catch my breath, so I skated outside of the rink and plopped down next to Leslie, who was sitting on the bench by the lockers.

"Are you going out there?" I asked.

"I'm chilling and enjoying the music."

"You didn't come here just to sit down, come on and skate." I caught a second wind and extended my hand to help Leslie into the rink. She wobbled a little but then steadied herself.

"Look." I pointed to a guy wearing a Rubik's Cube T-shirt and AJ jeans. "Isn't he cute? I'm going to give him my number."

"But Raven, you don't even know him."

I sucked my teeth. "Duh, that's why we're going to get each other's phone numbers."

The DJ started playing Nu Shooz's song "I Can't Wait," and the rink became packed with more kids and teenagers. We spotted our cousins skating in a trio and joined them. Together, all five of us skated around the rink in unison, with Champ taking the lead.

Champ leaned down and rode on one skate close to the floor. Everyone in the rink started cheering for him, but as soon as Champ did a spin move, we spun too far out and lost our grip on each other's hands. Lucci fell first, and Boogie landed on top of him. I tripped and landed on top of Boogie and Leslie fell on top of me. It was a train wreck.

Champ was in such a groove that he didn't realize we were no longer skating with him, even though we had let go of his hand. By the time he turned around, we were trying to get up off the floor without getting knocked over by oncoming traffic.

"Are you guys OK? What happened?" Champ extended his hand to pull Leslie up from the floor. Lucci, Boogie, and I had been trying to lift her up, but she kept falling back down.

"Get up, fatso."

When I looked over my shoulder, it was the cute guy in the Rubik's Cube T-shirt. He started taunting Leslie as he skated by. Each time he came around the rink, he called Leslie names as she kept slipping out of Champ's hands and falling to the floor.

"Stand up, Whopper butt."

"What did he say?" Lucci and Champ took a fighter's stance with their fists at their sides. Little Boogie even stepped forward like he was ready to fight too.

"Stay out of the rink, fat girl," the boy teased.

"Let's get that bamma!" Lucci pointed him out. He, Champ, and Boogie skated fast to catch up with the boy. They grabbed him and clobbered him with their fists.

"No, stop! Don't fight." Leslie howled over the top of the music, as she finally managed to keep her balance on her skates without falling again.

The referee blew his whistle loudly and broke up the fight. The cute boy left Crystal's Skating Rink crying since he got beat up. We thought the whole scene was hilarious, but Leslie didn't think it was funny. The referee made Champ, Lucci, and Boogie turn in their skates for the night. We chilled out in the food court until my mother came and got us.

"God doesn't like violence," Leslie said between sips of her Slurpee.

"God doesn't expect us to be punks either. You gotta stand up for yourself, Leslie," Champ told her, sounding like one of his basketball coaches.

"But Grandma said to walk away from ignorant people."

"I did walk away, right after I punched his lights out." Champ laughed, and he and the boys gave each other a high five.

"You better hope God forgives you, Champ." Leslie shook her head in disappointment.

"Cheer up, Cuz. We did the right thing." Champ placed his arm over Leslie's shoulder. "You're my cousin and don't nobody mess with my family. I got y'all backs always, and I will never let anything happen to you guys."

Mom picked us up at six, and we piled up in her car like sardines and drove to Iverson Mall. We bought sugar cookies, music, and books for Leslie to cheer her up. Afterward, Mom took us to Erol's video store down the street.

At Erol's, Boogie grabbed *Beat Street* on VHS, Champ and Lucci agreed on *The Terminator,* and Leslie and I picked *Valley Girl*. While at the counter, Lucci had asked the video clerk about his cousin Turk on his mom's side.

"Turk? I'm sorry, but I don't think we have an employee here by that name," the clerk replied, packing VHS movies in a big yellow plastic bag.

"His real name is Tyrone Timothy Jakes," I interrupted.

"Be quiet, girl. Don't be telling my cousin's government name!" Lucci shoved me.

"Don't push me!" I shoved him back. "Anyway, he's about this tall and he wears his hair in a box Philly haircut like Rakim from Eric B. and Rakim the rap group."

"Sorry, he no longer works here."

"Why? Did he get fired?" I asked.

"I'm not allowed to say," the clerk replied, eyes shaking and looking nervous.

"Please excuse my nosy daughter and nephew." Mom pulled us away from the counter. "Come on guys, let's go and quit asking people questions that's none of your business."

Once we got back to the house, we popped Jiffy popcorn and sat in front of the TV to watch our first movie, *The Terminator*. After all, Champ insisted.

Leslie and I were ready to watch our movie. Leslie was more patient than me. I couldn't take anymore shoot-'em-up and bang-bang, so I stood in front of the TV.

"Hey guys, why don't we make a pact?" I suggested.

"Move out the way, metal mouth," Lucci cracked on me.

"Don't be jealous. At least one day I will have a beautiful smile like Jayne Kennedy."

"Today ain't that day, move it." Champ shoved me out of the way.

"What kind of pact are you talking about?" Boogie asked.

"I think what Raven means is that we should make a promise," Leslie explained. She stood up from the sofa and paused the VCR. "Raven, say the promise you want us to make."

"'From this day forward, we are together forever.'" I repeated a line I'd heard on TV.

"That's so corny." Champ burst into laughter. "How about, 'Blood over water, no other relationship before us.'"

"I like that," Leslie agreed. "Let's put our hands together and make the promise."

"Blood over water, no other relationship before us," we

said in unison with our hands stacked on top of each other.

"I love you guys," I said, feeling tears form in my eyes. My cousins were like the brothers and the sister that I never had.

"We love you too," Leslie smiled.

"Group hug?" I opened my arms.

"Nah, that's enough of all that mushy stuff." Champ walked away and un-paused the movie.

"Yeah, let's finish watching the *Terminator*." Lucci sat back down next to Champ.

Me, Boogie, and Leslie decided to play a game of Uno. I happened to look up as my mother appeared in the living room in a sexy red dress and high heels.

"I'm going out with my girlfriends to see the Frankie Beverly & Maze show at Blues Alley," she said, and our eyes lit up in amazement at her beauty. "Leslie, you are in charge. I have my beeper if you need me."

"No problem," Leslie said. "You look very pretty, Aunt Diane."

"You think so?" Mom blushed a smile as she pulled her spaghetti strap purse over her shoulder.

"Yes!" we all said in unison.

"Thank you, guys. Now, be sure to behave yourselves and listen to Leslie."

"But I'm the oldest," Champ reminded her.

Mom pursed her lips. "Whatever, boy. Like I said, Leslie is in charge."

As soon as Mom left, Boogie, Leslie, and I went upstairs to her room to play dress up. We loved trying on her fancy clothes, especially Boogie, who seemed to love trying to walk in her high heels. Leslie and I laughed when his ankles wobbled, and he fell to the floor.

"I'll get it right one day," Boogie sighed.

"You will," I assured him. "One day, you and I will do a fashion show and catwalk for Ebony Magazine."

Boogie's lips formed a big smile. "Yes, that will be awesome!"

CHAPTER 5
SUMMER RAIN

LESLIE

Raindrops tap danced on our rooftop, providing a soundtrack to my new romance book, *Daisies in the Sand*. I was snuggled on the sofa in a pink hand-knitted blanket Grandma had made for me when I was a little girl. In the book, Paul had just confessed his love to Isabella, and they began to kiss passionately. Paul gently eased Isabella down on the wet sandy beach, and I imagined I was Isabella. Instantly, my skin flooded with warmth as my eyes rolled across each word in anticipation of what was about to happen next.

"What are you reading?"

My body jerked in shock from Grandma's voice, and the book fell to the floor. I quickly picked it up and clutched it to my chest, hiding the title with my hand.

"Uh...a story about people on the beach." I gulped.

"It's your turn to fix dinner for your mother." She walked off. I could hear her in the coat closet in the hallway.

I clucked my teeth, exhaled under my breath. "Shoot, I don't feel like cooking right now."

"Excuse me?"

Grandma stepped back into the living room. Obviously, she overheard me. I looked up from my book and she was standing in the living room wearing her yellow raincoat, yellow boots, and a yellow hat. If she had quacked, I would have thought she was Donald Duck.

"Don't forget to mind your manners, child." She looked at me sharply. "Come and lock the door behind me."

"Alright," I groaned.

"That's 'yes ma'am' to you," she corrected.

"But Aunt Diane said that saying *ma'am* and *sir* is old-fashioned."

"Your Aunt Diane has been a rebel since she came out the womb and snatched her umbilical cord back from the doctor."

I wrinkled my face. "Really?"

"No, child, but she *is* the one who got your mother in trouble in the first place. If she didn't...never mind." Grandma shook her head and grabbed her pocketbook from her favorite recliner by the living room window. That's when I noticed it was raining harder outside, making the windows look like blurred glass. It was Saturday night, and come rain, hail, sleet, snow, or even a tsunami, nothing was going to stop Grandma from going to play bingo with her friends.

"If Ms. Jean or Ms. Ann calls, tell them I will meet them at the van at the Safeway parking lot," she instructed as I followed her to the door.

Every Saturday, a Capitol Hill community van took the seniors in the neighborhood to Benning Road Recreation Center to play bingo. I locked the door and did a victory dance in celebration of Grandma leaving. "Now where was I?"

"Do you love me, Isabella?" Paul gazed into Isabella's eyes with flames of passion.

"Yes, I do love you Paul," Isabella said, teary-eyed.

"Will you marry me?"

KNOCK-KNOCK-KNOCK

"No way!" I tossed the blanket aside. Maybe these interruptions are a sign from God that I shouldn't be reading such a lusty book.

I went to the door and looked through the peephole. Mitch stood on the other side, drenched from the rain. His red and white Coca-Cola outfit was stuck to his tall frame. I wondered what he wanted, especially since Champ wasn't visiting today. He and Champ had developed an instant friendship through playing basketball at Watkins playground over the years. The two were now best friends.

"I know you're in there, Leslie. I can hear you breathing. Can you help me out?" Mitch spat through the pouring rain. He had a handsome, boyish look that all the girls in the neighborhood adored. He seemed to take their flirtatiousness with modesty. He'd always give off a nonchalant gaze and a half-smile as if he didn't know how attractive he was.

"I lost my keys, and I just need to use your phone to call my mother at work, if that's okay with you?" Mitch said, as the rain poured over him like a shower.

I unlocked the door, eased it open, and peeped my head around. "My grandmother said not to have company without her being home."

"But I can't get in my house. I got no place to go right now." He flopped his arms at his sides as a look of desperation appeared in his deep brown eyes. I opened the door wider and motioned my hand for him to come in. *So much for reading* Daisies in the Sand, I thought to myself.

"I'll grab a towel so you can dry off." I hurried upstairs as fast as I could and tried not to sound out of breath when I returned. Maybe my heavy breathing was part of my asthma or just being overweight or some combination of both, but I felt a little embarrassed from Mitch saying he could hear me breathing through the door.

As Mitch wiped off the rain, I noticed how smooth and tanned his skin looked. As he reached up to dry off his wet, wavy hair, I noticed the clusters of V-shaped scars on his wrists and grew concerned.

Mitch saw me staring and looked away, quickly tucking his hands into the pockets of his shorts. "Uh...can I use your phone?" He stuttered, nervously.

"Sure."

34

He followed me into the living room.

"Wow, I can't believe you guys still have this rotary phone," Mitch snickered, dialing his mom. Grandma still hadn't switched to a touch-tone phone yet. Raven and I hated using it, especially when we would try to win concert tickets on the radio. We'd have to stick our fingers into each numbered hole and turn the dial until it clicked. We never won tickets. Folks with a touch-tone always got the win.

I sat back down on the sofa and dog-eared the page in my book, so I'd remember where I'd left off while Mitch talked to his mother.

I overheard Ms. Larson say, "Mitch, this is the third time you lost your keys. We will have to go to Frazier's hardware store and get another set made again."

Mitch replied, "I'm sorry, Ma," and ended with a sweet, "Love you too. I'll see you shortly."

Mitch turned toward me. "Hey, is it cool if I hang out here until my mom gets off work?"

"Uhm, I guess it's OK." I shrugged. "Does your mother still work as a nurse at Greater Southeast?"

"Yep," he said, walking over to the TV.

"I hope she doesn't get off too late. Grandma doesn't permit me to have male company when she's not at home," I mention again to let him know I could get in trouble.

"I won't be here long. My mom gets off a little early tonight. Say, how do I turn this thing on?"

"Grandma said not to turn on the TV during a thunderstorm, but when it stops, you can use those pliers sitting next to it since Champ accidentally broke the knob."

Mitch turned from the TV and sat right next to me on the sofa with his hands clutched tightly together. We sat in silence for the next few minutes as the thunder outside sounded like bowling balls going down the lane. His eyes darted over the room, I could tell he didn't know what to talk about and I didn't either. It was my first time alone with a boy.

"So, how did you lose your keys?" I asked, breaking the silence between us.

"I was running from a group of guys from Kentucky Courts," he explained. "I think my keys must've fallen out of my pocket."

"Why were you running from them?"

"They were going to jump me."

"At least you got away."

"I normally don't run from anybody, but it was about thirty of them and one of me."

"How did you get these scars?" I traced my fingertips over the translucent marks on his wrists. They felt like allergy hives only firmer. He pulled his hands away and shoved them into his pockets.

"You want to talk about what happened?" I asked as gently as I could.

Mitch didn't answer. He glared out the window as if he didn't want to talk about it, so we watched the rain until it slowed down and eventually floated away with the clouds. Next thing we knew, the sun was shining again. That's how summer rains were in DC. One minute it would storm and the next, the sun would come back out.

Mitch stood up and turned on the TV using the pliers. Thankfully, it wouldn't be much longer before our new TV from Fingerhut would arrive.

"You want some Kool-Aid?" I asked, as *Gimme a Break!* played on the TV. It was a repeat episode, and I knew it was getting ready to go off.

"I'll take some."

By the time I finished making the Kool-Aid and returned to the living room, the ending credits were scrolling on the TV.

"Here you go." I handed Mitch a glass of red Kool-Aid and turned the dial to Channel 7 to watch *Dynasty*.

"Hey, I thought you were a church girl? You watch this sleazy show?"

"It's not sleazy. It's entertaining."

He laughed lightly. "Sure you right."

I turned up the volume, and as soon as I sat back down, Dominique smacked Alexis.

"Oh no she didn't!" My mouth gaped open.

"Oh snap! These chicks get down like that?" Mitch's lips curved into a wide grin. "I may have to start watching *Dynasty* more than WWF." He rested his hands behind his head and crossed his long legs at the ankles to get more comfortable.

When the show ended, we sat at the dining room table and played a few hands of Tunk and Deuces Wild. I was sitting with my back toward the living room and Mitch sat across from me at the opposite end of the table so we couldn't see each other's cards in our hands. We started talking about our favorite movies, music, and our favorite foods. I found out Mitch and I had a few things in common. Our favorite color was purple, and we both loved Rocky Road ice cream, and listening to Go-Go and Rap music on 1450AM WOL radio station. We also talked about our favorite rap artists: Doug E. Fresh, Salt-N-Pepa, Whodini, and LL Cool J.

"And do you watch Friday Night videos?" I asked.

"Yep."

"No way! Who are your favorite singers to watch?"

"Hall and Oats, Peter Gabriel, and Van Halen. I love so many, what about you?" he asked, expressing the same enthusiastic surprise as me.

"I love all those guys, too. I also like Madonna, Boy George, and Guns and Roses."

Mitch's eyes pulled back.

"I know that's surprising, but I love all kinds of music." I shuffled the cards, and when I looked up as I dealt us a new hand, Mitch's mouth dropped in shock.

"Did I say something wrong?" I asked, noticing he suddenly looked startled more than surprised.

He pointed his finger, and I turned my head to look behind me.

"MAMA?" My body jerked. I didn't even hear her come down the stairs. She was standing behind me wearing a blue scarf, a pair of gray sweatpants, and her navy-blue

Howard University T-shirt. Her eyes were locked on Mitch like a foreign object. I assumed she was wondering why he was there.

"Mama, do you remember Mitch? He's our neighbor from across the street," I reminded her. I was sure she had seen him plenty of times from her bedroom window, and when he would visit when Champ was here. I wanted to put her mind at ease so she would stop staring at him with a perplexed look on her face.

Mitch uttered a faint "Hello" and waved his hand, but Mama said nothing. She stared at him for a moment, then quickly snatched the bag of potato chips off the table and started to devour them. I realized she was hungry, and I had forgotten to cook her something to eat.

"I'll be right back, Mitch." I put my cards face down on the table and got up to fix Mama something to eat. I made a quick grilled cheese sandwich with a can of tomato soup, so I could hurry and get Mama back upstairs. I knew Mitch must've felt uncomfortable with Mama staring at him. I wish she wouldn't do that to people.

"Come on, Mama, let's go upstairs so you can eat." I nudged my head as I held her tray of food in my hands. I wanted to kick myself for forgetting to feed her, but I hoped she forgave me.

As soon as I set the food down on Mama's food tray stand, I heard someone downstairs knocking on the door.

"Sit down and eat, Mama. I will be right back to check on you," I said, turning on her TV before I rushed out of the room and down the stairs.

I tried to catch my breath before I opened the door. I looked through the peephole and it was Ms. Larson. She stood on the other side in her nurse's uniform. Her blonde stringy hair draped her shoulders, and her blue eyes looked dark like she hadn't slept in days.

"Mitch, your mom is here!" I called for him as I opened the door. "Hello, Ms. Larson."

"Hi Leslie."

Mitch came to the door. "Hey Ma, I'll be right there in a sec."

His mother heaved an impatient sigh as she headed to their house across the street.

Mitch turned to me. "Thanks for letting me hang out," he said, and kissed me on the mouth. I was taken completely off guard.

"You're welcome." I held my fingers over my lips in disbelief as Mitch ran across the street. I closed the door and couldn't stop smiling. I had finally been kissed. It was better than reading about Paul and Isabella. My heart danced with joy and even more when I heard the phone ringing in the living room. Assuming it was Mitch, I rushed to answer it.

"Hello?" My voice floated in anxious anticipation.

"Hey Leslie, did you see Dominique slap the crap out of Alexis?"

I recognized that high-pitched, proper voice right away. I panicked, as my hand tried to steady the phone against my ear. How was I going to tell her that Mitch kissed me?

CHAPTER 6
HANGING UP

RAVEN

"Hello?" I shouted into the phone, thinking the line went dead.

"Oh, hey Raven, sorry I almost dropped the phone." Leslie cleared her throat. "But uhm...yes, I watched *Dynasty*. It was a good episode. Really good. Yep."

"Are you okay?" I asked in between popping bubbles with my gum and twirling a long string of my hair around my finger.

"Mitch just left," Leslie said, and her voice shook like she was nervous.

"Mitch? Why was he over there? Was Champ and Boogie visiting today or something?"

"No."

Something wasn't right. Leslie's short answer created an awkward moment of silence between us.

"Well then, is everything OK with Mitch?"

"We...I mean...*he* kissed me."

I sprung up out of the bed. "Wait, you kissed Mitchell Larson?"

"Yes. I mean. He kissed me."

"Like a peck kiss or a French kiss?"

"A peck kiss, but my mouth was kind of opened."

"How could you let him kiss you when you know I've been in love with him since I was nine years old?"

"I swear it's not my fault."

"Humph, well, did you like it?" I spat, feeling a tightness forming in my throat.

"Honestly? Yes, but I'm sorry, Raven. I didn't mean for any of this to happen."

"Did you forget our family promise? Blood over water, no other relationship before us?" I blinked back tears of hurt. Leslie's silence spoke volumes.

"So, I guess this means you guys are going steady now?"

"I guess so."

"Did you even tell Mitch that I liked him first?"

"Well, I—"

"Never mind. I don't want to hear any more of this!"

"Raven, I'm really sorry I—"

CLICK

I slammed the phone in her ear just as my mother walked into the room holding a laundry basket filled with cleaned clothes. She took one look at my red, fuming face and knew something was wrong.

"What's gotten you so upset?" she asked, her eyebrows lifted with curiosity more than concern, as she put my clothes away.

"Leslie kissed Mitch when she knew I liked him first."

"That's it?" Mom collapsed her arms at her side. "Girl, I thought something drastic happened."

"That *was* drastic, Mom!"

"I see it runs in the family."

I pouted and crossed my arms. "What do you mean?"

"Your Aunt Irene once kissed a guy I liked. As a matter of fact, they got engaged. Anyway, you'll get over it."

"No, I won't."

"You will, but just don't do anything crazy out of revenge like I did, or you may regret it later."

"I'm not that desperate."

"Good. There are plenty of other guys out there, and you and Leslie don't need to fight over one," she said, closing my door as she walked off.

I couldn't believe my own cousin went behind my back and stole my man. I'm never speaking to Leslie again!

CHAPTER 7
A LONG HOT SUMMER

LUCCI

I woke up to someone banging on our front door downstairs. A sheet of sweat covered my half-naked body as I made my way to the window. Through the broken blinds, I could see a fat lady in an orange floral dress banging on our door. Her brown Pinto hatchback was double-parked in the street, and three small children were inside.

"Willie Earl, I know you're in there!" the woman shouted.

I had a funny feeling she must have been Earl's wife, Mrs. Diggs. Leslie and I had found Earl's home number in my mother's phone book yesterday, while her and Earl had gone dancing at the Chateau. She pretended to be my mom and told Mrs. Diggs they were having an affair. It was fun having Leslie over, even though I didn't feel like I needed a sitter. My mom had called her to watch me since CPS had stopped by a couple of weeks ago. They warned mom not to leave me alone for more than a few hours. You see, sometimes I would be home by myself for hours without food. And if mom went on a binge, it would last for days. Anyway, I couldn't wait to tell Leslie that the prank worked.

I put on my striped Alligator shirt with the matching shorts that Champ had given to me, and sprinted downstairs to check out the action.

"...and you had better stay away from my husband, you scallywag winch!" Mrs. Diggs pointed a threatening finger at my mom.

I sat down on the bottom stairstep and watched the

42

scene unfold like a WWF wrestling match. Mom and Mrs. Diggs started fighting like two alley cats.

"What's going on down there?" Earl rushed down the stairs half-dressed, almost knocking me off the step. He tried to break up the fight and got whacked on the head. Eventually, he was able to break them up but not without getting scratched.

"If you want him, you can have him. I got plenty of other men, heifer!" Mom shouted.

"Willie Earl, I swear if you don't get dressed and leave this house with me right now, you won't ever see your children again," Mrs. Diggs threatened.

Earl stood in the middle of the two of them, looking like he was trying to decide what to do next. Reluctantly, Earl grabbed his shoes from under the living room table, put them on, and left with Mrs. Diggs.

"I don't need him anymore, anyway." Mom scowled as she flopped down on the sofa. She didn't look happy about what had just happened.

"Mom, are you sure you're going to be okay?" I asked, sitting down next to her. I gently took hold of her hand. It was a gesture that Leslie and Grandma always did with me.

"Boy don't touch me!" she snatched her hand back like I had leprosy.

"Dang, I was just trying to be nice."

"Nice? You can be nice by going over to your grandmother's house and getting out of my face. That's how your beady headed behind can be nice."

"Well, I ain't going over there yet. I just woke up."

"Don't get sassy with me. Besides, it's after two o'clock. You're usually outside washing cars or something," she sneered, grabbing the TOP paper off the coffee table to roll up a joint.

"That's why Mrs. Diggs beat you up," I mumbled.

"What did you say?"

I clinched my jaw and grumbled, "Nothing."

43

Just then, we heard keys unlocking the door. I hoped it wasn't Earl coming back since he didn't return Mom's keys.

The door swung open, Turk stepped inside wearing an all-navy Fila short set and brand-new white Fila shoes to match.

"Are y'all okay?" Turk's eyes bucked like he was on a hunt to find the trouble.

"Yeah, we're good." I flexed my arms and fists like I was a big man who could protect me and my mother.

"I was just up the block when a little birdie told me something was popping off down here."

"Lucci said we're good, didn't he?" Mom rolled her eyes.

"Don't get smart with me."

"Whatever. I need to be alone. Can you take Lucci to his grandmother's house?" Mom asked in a demanding tone.

"Alright let's make this quick, I'm supposed to meet somebody in twenty minutes to handle business. Lucci, go upstairs and get dressed."

I frowned up my nose. "But I am dressed."

Turk's eyes stared me up and down. "What happened to the Adidas sweatsuit and new shoes your Aunt Diane bought you? You can't wear penny loafers with that outfit."

"This is all I got left. My mother stole everything else, including the pennies I put in these loafers. And she took my Mello Yellow soda jug with my car washing money."

"We needed food in this house and the phone bill needed to be paid too." Mom jerked up from the sofa to plead her case. "Every time your father calls here collect, it goes up another hundred dollars."

"That ain't the only thing you used the money for. It's this dope you smoke!" I knocked over the ashtray.

"Boy, you better pick it up!" Mom yelled, and I reluctantly grabbed it off the floor.

"Theresa, you ain't have to do that boy like that."

"Don't tell me what to do!" Mom shouted. "You make enough money to get us out of this dump but we're still here, so don't keep coming around here barking orders. I don't work for you no more."

"I help pay the rent, don't I?" Turk crossed his arms.

"Negro, the rent ain't but fifty dollars."

Turk bit down on his lip and shook his head in frustration. "I just gave you four hundred dollars two weeks ago. What happened to it? Did it go up your nose or through your veins?"

Mom cocked her head to the side. "Don't judge me when it's dealers like you who got us all hooked in the first place."

"You used to be one of us, but you forgot the number one rule," Turk pointed. "Never get high off your own supply."

Mom dragged one last puff from her joint and blew the smoke in Turk's face.

Turk gave her a hard shove. "You better watch yourself, girl! Don't you forget who's the boss," he told her sternly.

"Only boss of mine was Aunt Gloria." Mom scoffed, as she sat back down on the sofa.

"Well, I'm running things now." Turk thumped his chest with his hand. "I got every ghetto around here on lock. Soldiers in Capers, Potomac Gardens, and Kentucky Courts all report to me—the H.N.I.C. I'm trying to put you back on so you can take care of Lucci, but you can't stay clean for five minutes."

"I would still be in the game if that cheap condom ain't pop. A kid wasn't part of my plans."

"Hold up, you ain't want me?" I interjected, springing up from the sofa to face her.

"Nope, sure didn't," Mom finished off her joint, leaving the roach in the ashtray. "I only screwed your father to find out who his connection was."

"Why would you say something like that to your kid?" Turk's eyes pulled back in shock.

"She's an evil witch that's why!" I felt so angry that my skin felt hot. I lost it and flipped the coffee table over.

"Boy, you better respect me in my own house. Pick it up!"

"I ain't picking nothing up!"

She jumped up from the sofa and grabbed me by the shirt.

"Stop it! Let him go, Tee." Turk yanked her hands off me, and I ran outside to his car. The neighbors on the block stopped to see what was going on. They watched as Turk and mom loudly exchanged words in the doorway until Turk threw his hands up in the air, giving up on the argument. There was no reasoning with mom. She didn't care about anybody, not even me.

I climbed into the car with Turk, blinking back angry tears so Turk wouldn't see them forming in my eyes. I never felt so unwanted in all my life.

Turk sped off from the curb, shaking his head angrily and complaining about my mother. I couldn't blame him.

"...and another thing," Turk was saying. "I don't think you should go back there."

"If I can't go back home, can I stay with you?" I asked softly. My heart felt sad.

"What?" Turk turned the radio volume down. Robbie Nevil was singing, "C'est Le Vie."

"I said, can I stay with you?"

"Nah shorty. I got a rule that no one needs to know where I live. If they don't know, they can't tell the cops. Besides, I'm barely at home," he said, putting the pedal to the metal like he was in a hurry. He almost ran through a red light."

I groaned. "Nobody wants me."

"That ain't true."

"I can't live with you, and I can't live with my mom, and my father is in jail. Who else I got?" I sniffed, swallowed down salty tears.

"The Walker family cares about you, and you should always go where there is love."

"You don't love me?"

"Of course I do, but right now I'm in the streets," he said, checking each car mirror as if he was looking out for the cops. "Despite what your mother said, she loves you too."

I twisted my lips. "Man, you must think I'm stupid. She don't love me."

"Your mother is sick right now that's all."

"But even when she's not on drugs she acts so mean to me."

"I'll try to get her back in rehab, but not the one at DC General," he said. "Too many of her friends are there. Maybe in the right facility she'll come back and be a better mother to you."

"I want to make my own money and move away. Let me work a corner for you. I already know you don't work at Erol's anyway."

Turk rubbed his chin. "Nah man, the streets ain't for you."

"But I need money to survive out here."

"You ain't ready for this life. A hustler never sleeps. We always gotta watch our backs."

"So what, I can watch my back."

"It's more to it than that. You gotta have quick thinking and be able to see the smoke before the fire. It's like a chess match out here not checkers."

"Then why don't you teach me?"

Turk heaved a deep sigh and winced his eyes with a curious stare. "Hmmm...maybe one day, but right now you're only thirteen."

"My friend Dre said he hustles for you, and he's just fourteen."

"I'll think about it, but you tell Dre if he wants to keep working for me don't mention my name again."

We pulled up in front of grandma's house. Turk reached into his sock and pulled out a wad of money wrapped in a rubber band. My eyes lit up with excitement, but then Turk peeled off two twenty-dollar bills instead of giving me the larger bills from the stack.

"Buy yourself a new pair of shoes."

"Shoes? What about clothes? I told you my mother stole everything."

Turk gave me the side eye. "And you wonder why I call you Lucci? You always need more money for something.

Anyway, I guess I can't have you out here looking like a bum."

Turk peeled off six fifty-dollar bills.

"Wow! Three-hundred dollars! Thanks, Turk."

"No sweat. You got my beeper number, right?"

"Yep."

"Page me if you ever need anything. Gimme dabs." Turk and I did a quick fist bump.

I wasn't sure when I'd see Turk again, but I knew if I wanted to survive, I needed to find my own hustle. I didn't want to be somebody's charity case.

CHAPTER 8
SUMMER MADNESS

RAVEN

I was singing along with Eddy Grand's "Electric Avenue," as I slowly stringed the mozzarella cheese around the tip of my tongue. My parents and I were sitting in a booth at Shaky's pizza. The music played from a jukebox in the corner. Dad gave me an awkward stare and heaved a long sigh.

"Pumpkin are you almost finished?" he asked.

"No, not yet." I said, chewing extra slow and taking tiny bites of the last slice of pepperoni pizza.

"You need to hurry up." Mom glared at me and crossed her arms. They finished their pizza a half hour ago.

Dad glanced at his watch and his expression turned stony-faced. The waitress approached our table for the third time, asking if we needed anything else.

"Can I see the dessert menu?" I asked.

"We won't be needing a menu, just ring us up for a brownie to go please," Dad said to the waitress.

"But we always eat the dessert together." I groaned, swallowing a lump of cheese in my throat, as the waitress walked back to the kitchen.

"You shouldn't have taken so long to eat dinner," Mom snapped. "Your father has a plane to catch, and I have to prepare for a case when I get home."

I sulked in disappointment and let my body slouch down in the booth seat.

"Raven, there's something your mother and I need to talk to you about," Dad said in a tone that indicated I wasn't going to like what was coming next.

My heart couldn't bear any more bad news. It was depressing enough that Leslie and Mitch had kissed two weeks ago. Even though Leslie said they hadn't talked since then, I still wished it were me.

"Well, what is it?" I slightly pouted my lips, not really wanting to hear what was coming next.

Dad reached across the table and rested his hand on top of mine. "Sweetheart, this isn't easy for us to tell you, but—"

"Your father and I are officially divorced, is what he's trying to say."

"Darn it, Diane! You didn't have to say it like that." Dad slammed his hand on the table.

The waitress came over with a clear container with a brownie inside. She could sense the tension, and politely sat the box on the table with the tab next to it.

"Uhm...no rush on the bill. Whenever you're ready, you can take it to the cashier," she hurried off.

"Must you be so blunt *all* the time?" Dad shook his head at Mom, who was sitting next to him.

"Raven doesn't need a sympathy speech, so why drag it out?"

"I don't want to hear this! I hate you both!" I stood up so abruptly that my knee hit the table and rattled the utensils.

"Sweetheart, wait!" Dad tried to grab my hand, but I rushed out of the dining area and down the hall to the ladies' room.

Thankfully, no one was in the restroom, and I cried my eyes out. As I stood before the mirror above the sink, my entire face had flushed red like a cherry.

"It's your fault!" I shouted at my reflection.

The restroom door slowly opened, and Mom walked in with a blasé facial expression. She had sort of a smirk, like this was some joke.

"Girl, I know you are not crying," she mocked. "You knew this day was coming. Your father and I have been separated since you were nine years old."

"I thought when Dad stayed the night with you last week that you were finally getting back together."

"Humph, is that what you thought?" She twisted her lips. "Honey, nothing went well that night. It was a small fire that quickly flamed out before we could even turn off the lights. That's how we knew it was over between us."

"But I promise I'll be better in school, and I won't ask for money to buy so many things anymore."

Mom propped her hands on her hips and tilted her head as her eyebrows drew inward. "Raven, this isn't about you. You are *not* the cause of our divorce."

"Well, I thought marriage was supposed to be happily ever after."

"I shouldn't have allowed you to watch those fairy-tale movies." She chuckled, but I didn't find anything funny. "The truth is, we grew apart a long time ago. We are two different people. We're not the same couple we were in college. When you get older, you will understand what I mean."

"Grandma said you have a mouth like a pit bull. I'm thinking she's right."

"I beg your pardon! Don't you dare speak to me that way, young lady," she bellowed.

"I hate you!" I stormed out of the restroom. Mom was hot on my heels, shouting that I was a spoiled brat, as I hurried out of Shaky's Pizza.

"Diane, let me handle this." Dad rushed up to me as I approached his black Mercedes in the parking lot. He always drove his Benz instead of his Porsche when he had more than two passengers.

"Now Pumpkin, I know you're upset." Dad wrapped his arms around me. "It's going to be alright."

"No, it's not. You're leaving us!" I cried. "This is so unfair."

"*Shhh*...it's okay, sweetie. I'm never going to leave you." Dad stroked the top of my head.

"Girl, get your behind in the car and quit acting like a two-year-old. You're thirteen years old, so stop it." Mom rolled her eyes.

Dad opened the car door, and I stepped into the backseat and slammed the door shut. When my parents got in, they started arguing back and forth. I couldn't understand how two people who used to be in love now hated each other. After a while, the arguing stopped only because Dad refused to talk about it anymore. Mom had to have the last word.

"...and you had better make sure the child support and alimony checks arrive on time or I'll have your narrow behind right back in court," Mom said sharply, rolling her neck.

Dad simply shook his head and turned up the radio dial. Patti LaBelle and Michael McDonald sang "On My Own," but for me, it was bad timing. The tears streamed down my cheeks even more.

The next day, I ran away to teach my parents a lesson. Normally, whenever I left home, I had to call my parents at work and let one of them know where I was going to hang out. This time, I decided they weren't worth the call. I used my allowance money and took a taxi from our house in Clinton to Champ and Boogie's house in Temple Hills, which was about a fifteen-minute ride. The metro bus would've taken longer.

When the cab pulled up outside of Champ and Boogie's split-level home, I didn't see Uncle Henry's Bronco parked in the driveway. I got out and rang the doorbell anyway. The taxi driver with a cartoonish face like Mario from *Mario Brothers* yelled out the window, "I need to get going if someone isn't home."

I gritted my teeth, turned around, and rang the doorbell one more time. Finally, I heard someone unlocking the door. Aunt Naomi's head appeared in the crack of the door. Her red hair was rolled with big green rollers, and she was wearing a robe like I'd just woken her up. Her freckled face squinted against the bright sun.

"Raven? What are you doing here?"

"Uhm..." I didn't know what to say. In my mind, I had it all planned out for Champ or Boogie to answer the door, not their mom. I looked over my shoulder and watched the taxi speed off. I had paid him ten dollars, so he could've left me minutes ago if he wanted to.

"Come on inside." Aunt Naomi motioned her hand. "Did your mother or father send you here in a taxi? Are they okay?"

"No, but can I stay here for a few days?" I let my small suitcase drop to my feet.

"Raven, what's going on?" Aunt Naomi's eyes narrowed on the suitcase and then at me.

I explained to her about my parents' divorce and not wanting me. I was hoping she would give me a sympathetic ear like Leslie did when I had called to tell her that my parents had divorced.

"Raven, have you lost your mind? Running away never solves anything. It only makes matters worse. I bet your parents must be worried sick about you." Aunt Naomi went into the living room to grab the phone. She immediately dialed their numbers, but when neither of them answered, I wasn't surprised.

"I'll try them back shortly. Have a seat." Aunt Naomi directed me to the chair by the fireplace, and she sat across from me on the sofa. Guilt about what I had done began to sink in and I dropped my chin to my chest.

"When your Uncle Henry and the boys get back from Champ's AAU game, I'm going to have him take you back home where you belong. You do have your keys, right?"

I nodded my head a slow yes.

"I didn't mean to snap at you, Raven, it must be my hormones." She patted her belly.

"Wait, you're having a baby?" I asked, remembering how in school they taught us the changes in a woman's hormones when she became pregnant.

"We're waiting until the Fourth of July to announce it to the whole family at the reunion."

"Congratulations."

"Thank you, Raven. Doc says it may be a girl this time. Champ and Boogie are already excited. They can't wait to welcome her."

"Me too. Having a girl cousin will be so much fun. It's always been just me and Leslie."

"I agree. Would you like something to eat or to drink before I go get dressed?" Aunt Naomi stood up from the sofa.

"I'm not hungry, but Aunt Naomi..."

"Yes?"

"I hope I didn't hurt the baby by worrying you."

"You didn't hurt the baby at all. We will sort things out and get you back home where you belong."

"Okay."

When Aunt Naomi went upstairs to get dressed, I walked over to the fireplace and admired Champ's trophies on the mantel. My eyes shifted to their new family portrait to the right. I smiled at how happy they looked together and wished my parents were still together, too. Maybe we would be one happy family.

Then again, maybe not. My parents were always arguing with each other. They could hardly hold a conversation without fussing. I remembered the day my dad said he was moving out. The three of us were supposed to go skiing in Aspen, but they'd gotten into an argument about money, and Dad cancelled the whole trip. When they separated, Dad would pick me up occasionally and take me shopping, and every few months we ate dinner together as a family. Now that they're divorced, we'll probably never have dinner together again. Maybe I wanted us together more than they ever wanted to be.

Uncle Henry and my cousins came home an hour later, and they were just as surprised to see me as Aunt Naomi was. Aunt Naomi told Uncle Henry what had happened, and he quickly hurried me to his Bronco to take me home. Boogie and Champ sat in the backseat with me. I sat in the middle of them.

I started crying as I realized the magnitude of my decision to run away. I knew I was going to get into serious trouble this time.

Boogie took hold of my hand as the three of us rode to my house in silence. Boogie didn't say anything, but his upper eyelids were pulled up so high that I knew he was scared. I was scared for me, too.

Champ looked at me with his upper lip raised, like he was bothered. "Crying is for wimps."

"I'm not a wimp!"

"You better ask to go to the bathroom. And when you go in there, stuff some toilet paper in your pants so it won't hurt." He broke out in laughter that sounded spiteful.

I didn't think it was funny. I was so scared my hands started trembling. Leslie was right. When I told her I was going to run away she said it was a stupid idea. I didn't want to listen to her because I was still angry that she and Mitch had kissed.

When I got home, there wasn't enough time for me to go to the bathroom and prepare like Champ had advised.

"Do what you need to do, sis," Aunt Naomi told my mother, as we stood in the doorway like I was a lost-and-found puppy.

As soon as they said their goodbyes, Mom turned toward me with her cheeks puffed and lips pulled tight. Her eyebrows turned downward into a menacing look as she rolled up her sleeves. Without hesitating, I took off running upstairs, and this made Mom angrier. Mom caught me at the top of the stairs and let me have it. She reminded me that I was not grown.

I knew not to ever run away again.

CHAPTER 9
CRUEL SUMMER

LESLIE

August 14, 1986

Dear Diary,

I really wish Mitch would kiss me again. He barely looks at me whenever he's hanging out or playing ball with my cousins. I wonder if he feels embarrassed by it, and if it's because I'm fat. Today it's partly cloudy outside. I hope it's going to rain. Every time it rains, I think about Mitch again.

Last month was the Walker family reunion at Hains Point. Uncle Henry and Aunt Naomi proudly announced they were expecting a girl. That explained why Aunt Naomi had eaten Grandma's whole jar of spicy pickles.

We played volleyball, horseshoe, kickball, and baseball. We also took family photos in front of "The Awakening," a 72-foot statue of a giant man coming out of the ground. I wished Mama could've been there. Our neighbor, Ms. Jean, kept an eye on Mama while we were gone. Mama didn't like to go outside. It was a terrifying experience for her. Each time Grandma tries to take her outside to get some fresh air, Mama would run back into the house. She missed all the fun at the reunion.

By sunset, we lit fireworks and watched volcanos of

beautiful colors launch into the sky. Since then, Champ and Boogie's parents had been dropping them off to hang out with us while they went to work. Aunt Naomi was teaching summer school at Hine just blocks away from our house, and Uncle Henry worked a beat near Union Station less than ten minutes from us. Raven had also been staying the night at our house all week since her mother was away on work-related travel.

When she dropped off Raven, there was an older looking man with a beard in the driver's seat. Raven said his name was Gerald, and they were coworkers. They seemed like more than that if you ask me. There was something about the way their cheeks blushed at each other when they were dropping off Raven. I didn't mind Raven's company, but I wished she'd pitch in and help with household chores.

As for Lucci, he lives with us now and stays in the basement. I overheard Grandma telling my aunts how she tried to get public assistance for Lucci, but when she called Theresa asking to get custody, she told Grandma no and hung up the phone. She said Theresa won't give up custody of Lucci because she gets a monthly welfare check for him and she spends it on herself. Aunt Diane and Uncle Henry help whenever they can, and Aunt Diane said when she gets back in town, she will help Grandma file legal paperwork to get custody of Lucci.

At least Lucci's dad cares about him, even though his mother doesn't. He calls collect once a month and writes. He was locked up in Lorton, but due to overcrowding, they shipped him all the way to Texas. We hadn't seen Uncle Donovan since we were little kids. I feel sorry for Uncle Donovan. He often states how much he misses the family in his letters, and that the only person who visited him in Texas was Uncle Henry. Grandma says she is afraid to fly, and Aunt Diane claims she is too busy. I heard family rumors that Uncle Donovan had killed someone. Maybe the family is afraid to be around him, and Uncle Henry isn't since he's a police officer. All I know is that Uncle Donovan makes beautiful artistic greeting cards every year for me and my cousins' birthdays. I hope when he gets out, he will become an artist. Anyway, I need to finish doing our laundry. I will try to write sooner next time. Grandma is cooking yok with fried chicken tonight. It's our favorite. I'm hungry and can't wait to eat. Until later...

-Leslie

"Touchdown!" Raven shouted from the porch steps, sounding like the cheerleader she was for her school. Champ had just scored to tie the game and did a bragging victory dance. Lucci punted the ball back to Boogie and Mitch. Boogie caught the ball. He was small but quick. We watched him zigzag around Lucci and sprint past him to try to score a touchdown. A touchdown meant running to the stop sign on the corner.

"Go Boogie!" Raven and I cheered for him from the porch steps.

Mitch tried to block Champ so Boogie could run past him to score a touchdown, but Champ broke loose from Mitch's grip and ran after Boogie. He grabbed him by the shirt before he reached the stop sign.

"Get off me, you cheated!" Boogie pulled himself out of Champ's grip.

"No, I didn't cheat. You're just mad because I caught you," Champ retorted.

Boogie stomped back down the street, cursing Champ under his breath as he rejoined his partner, Mitch, in the middle of the street.

"Don't sweat it. We'll score on the next run." Mitch patted Boogie on the head. Boogie grabbed the football and kicked it in a haphazard fashion, causing the ball to roll underneath a parked car.

"Boogie, stop acting like a little punk and kick the ball right," Champ demanded.

"I'm not a sissy!"

"I never called you a *sissy*, but you're acting like a crybaby," Champ teased.

Boogie shoved Champ. Champ pushed him back.

"Knock it off, guys. Grab the ball!" Mitch shouted, impatiently.

Champ walked away from Boogie to retrieve the ball. "Here, Shrimp, now kick it right this time."

"Don't call me Shrimp!" Boogie dropped the ball and charged into Champ with his fist.

"Chill out, Boogie. I always call you Shrimp. What's wrong you today?" Champ put up his arms to block Boogie's punches. "Cut it out Boogie before you make me hit you back."

"Oh, come on, quit horsing around and let's finish the game!" Mitch shouted.

"Yeah, come on. I don't have all day," Lucci added.

"Cut it out, guys!" I shouted from the steps. I was tired and didn't have the energy to break up any fights today. The boys were always scuffling one minute, then playing the next.

Champ grabbed Boogie's hands to make him stop throwing punches. "If I let you go, you had better behave. I'm not going to warn you again."

Boogie wouldn't let up. He spat in Champ's face, and Champ lost it. He punched Boogie in the face, knocking him to the ground, but Boogie quickly rose to his feet and took a fighter's stance.

"Is that all you got?" Boogie challenged, and the two of them went for blows.

"Get out the street y'all, a truck is coming!" Lucci yelled, as he and Mitch ran out of the street onto the sidewalk. Champ and Boogie were too engaged in fighting to notice.

Buurrnp. The loud horn tooted from the truck.

"WATCH OUT!" I shouted at Champ and Boogie, as Raven and I ran down the porch steps, waving our arms in the air and yelling for the driver to stop. He tooted his horn again.

Boogie, who could see the truck coming, stopped throwing punches at Champ, and jumped out of the way. Champ, who had his back turned, didn't see the truck until it was too late. His eyes bucked with fear and in a split second, the front bumper of the truck smacked into Champ with so much force that all we heard was a loud *thump*. The impact of the hit sent Champ flying into the air, and as he came down, his head slammed into the hood of the truck and his body smacked into the asphalt.

"OH MY GOD!" Raven screamed.

"NOOOOO!" I wailed.

We all ran into the street, including neighbors who happened to be sitting on their front porches. The driver, who was a beer-bellied White man with a weird comb-over, approached the front bumper reeking of alcohol.

"Hey kid, are you OK? Didn't you hear me blowing the horn?" The man was swaying side to side like he was trying to keep his balance. He was clearly drunk.

"What happened?" Grandma came rushing out of the house upon hearing the commotion. A look of horror came over her face when she caught sight of Champ, whose ligaments were bent every which way, and his sneakers were halfway across the street.

"I'm going to call an ambulance!" Raven hurried into the house while Grandma leaned down next to Champ.

"Help is on the way, baby," she cried, as she stroked the side of his cheek with her hand.

"Everything will be alright, Champ." I took hold of his free hand, and it felt limp and cold.

Boogie kneeled next to his brother on the ground. "I'm sorry Champ. Please get up. You have an AAU Championship game tomorrow."

Champ's lips quivered as if he was trying to say something, and then his eyes rolled into the back of his head.

"No, no, no, stay with us, baby." Grandma kept patting his other hand.

Seeing the crowd's shocking reaction to Champ seemed to make the driver turn from being sympathetic to angry.

"These darn kids shouldn't have been playing in the streets." The driver tugged at the side of his hair in frustration. A Black lady with a blonde wig climbed out of the passenger seat of the truck. She walked toward the front of the truck, and upon seeing Champ on the ground, her head jerked to the side, and she threw up.

"You five-dollar trick! This is your fault!" the driver yelled at the woman as she upchucked.

"Mom?" Lucci's jaw dropped in shock. The woman's familiar brown eyes glared at him, then she took off running down an alley. That's when I realized the woman wearing the blonde wig was Theresa. She was so skinny and dirty I hardly recognized her.

I turned my attention back to Champ, whose face was starting to turn blue and swell like a whale in water. My stomach tightened with fear as I watched my cousin struggle to hold on to life.

"Don't go, Champ. We need you!" Lucci cried as Mitch rubbed his shoulders, trying to console him, but he was crying too.

The sound of sirens cut through the air, and when I looked up, police patrol cars and an ambulance were fast approaching. Champ's neck limped to the side and a stream of blood fell from the corner of his mouth. I didn't feel his pulse anymore and when I looked at his face, his eyes went someplace else, like how Mama's eyes would look, except Champ's stopped moving.

Everything seemed like slow motion, as if I were inside of a movie. The EMT hopped out of the ambulance. Uncle Henry, who was in one of the police patrol cars with Aunt

Naomi, pushed onlookers aside to get to Champ. We watched in angst as the EMT tried to resuscitate Champ. Grandma squeezed Aunt Naomi's hand, and the two of them prayed aloud. After several minutes, the EMTs shook their heads, and I watched their lips utter words that no one wanted to hear.

"I'm sorry, but...he's gone."

My body suddenly felt numb, as if a part of me had left with Champ. I couldn't believe just moments ago my cousin was innocently playing football, and in the blink of an eye he was gone. I couldn't talk. I couldn't move. I didn't know what to say or what to do next.

It was a cruel summer day in 1986.

CHAPTER 10
I MISS YOU

BOOGIE

My big brother Henry "Champ" Walker Jr. was dead. It was my fault. Leslie held me in her arms at the funeral home as tears streamed down both of our cheeks. A picture of Champ wearing his red and blue DeMatha varsity jacket sat on an easel in front of the stage. He was smiling with a basketball propped in his lap.

Every time I looked at it, I felt worse. It made me feel like he was looking at me. I just wanted to tell him I was sorry.

Next to the easel, Champ's body lay cold in an all-white casket. He looked like he was sleeping, except his eyes weren't blinking. Raven and Aunt Diane had helped my mother choose the gray pinstriped suit he was wearing. I thought it looked nice. There was a long line of people waiting to get a close view of him, including his former classmates, teammates, coaches, neighbors, and girlfriends he had over the years.

Each time someone looked at him in the casket, they walked away crying. Maybe because he looked like a plastic mannequin. I knew he wouldn't have approved of the pinkish color the funeral parlor put on his lips. In the corners of the funeral home were news reporters with badges around their necks and notepads in their hands. I didn't realize how popular my brother was until now.

After the viewing of the body, a Pastor gave a sermon about Champ, and then Dad took the stage with tears flowing down his cheeks. He began to talk about Champ with so much affection that you would have thought Champ was his only son. He was still angry at me. I told him Champ and I had been fighting the day he was killed. He got mad and whipped my behind. I deserved it this time.

Dad was also angry with the media who had written about Champ. The heading read: "Local High School Basketball Player Killed by Drunk Driver." Dad was upset that the article was only a few sentences. As he took the podium at the funeral home, he looked at each corner into the faces of the reporters.

"My son was more than just a few words in a newspaper," he said. "I'm going to tell you what the papers should have said about my son. Hopefully you guys get it right this time."

I pulled out the handkerchief from my suit pocket and blew my runny nose. The way Dad snarled his upper lip at me from the podium, I realized it was too loud.

"My Champ was an honor roll student," Dad continued. "He was competitive in everything he did. Winning in life gave him a sense of accomplishment. I raised him to do his best or not do it at all. Colleges were not only looking at him as a ball player but as a smart academic student. He was a handsome fella, funny, and a bit of a prankster. His dream was to play for Duke with hopes of getting drafted to the Los Angeles Lakers. Unfortunately, we know what happened." Dad paused and dabbed his wet eyes with his handkerchief.

"I paid that drunken murderer, Theophilus Duckworth, a visit to his jail cell. I asked him why he didn't make a sharp turn and hit a tree instead of my son. He looked me square in the eyes and said, 'I honked my horn twice and he ignored it. He got what he deserved,'" Dad said, and the audience heaved a loud groan.

"My firstborn son, Henry Jr., once said that I was his hero..." Dad choked. "But little did he know...he was always mine."

The audience sighed and groaned. All I heard were

sniffles. I looked around and saw every face was wet with tears, even one of the reporters removed his glasses to wipe his eyes. My heart hurt. I wanted to take away everyone's pain. I wished I could snap my fingers and bring my brother back.

Dad sobbed. "See you in paradise my son. Rest on."

The funeral ended with a closing prayer, and everyone headed to our house for food.

Despite everyone offering their condolences, I still felt horrible for starting that fight with Champ. My cousins kept telling me not to blame myself, but I couldn't shake the guilt. I needed to figure out a way to fix what I had done.

PART 2

COMING OF AGE

CHAPTER 11
THE HULK IS OUT
DECEMBER 1989

LUCCI

I hated that I had to spend my sixteenth birthday at Oakhill Youth Detention Center, but my life hadn't been the same since Champ died. It was my idea to play football instead of basketball that day. I still feel like his death was partially my fault.

Over the past few years, my mother kept going in and out of rehab, and my grandmother got custody of me. Grandma said I drove her crazy with the trouble I kept getting into, from hooking school, getting into fights, and selling drugs for Turk. Whenever she complained I'd leave her some money and she'd be quiet until the next shenanigan I'd pull. One day she told my father, and he yelled at me on the phone.

"Turk ain't no good. He only thinks about himself. All the work I put in for him and your mother and not one time did they come and see me. I bet when you get locked up, they won't come and visit you either."

It was the same old spill every time he called, and frankly, ain't nothing he can tell me since he was locked up. I loved making money and being my own man. I was tired of wearing knock-off brand clothes from Morton's and no-name sneakers from thrift stores. Girls wanted dudes with jewelry, cars, money, and stylish clothes. When Turk finally gave me a corner, I bought everything I ever wanted, and booked all the fly honeys too. I got a Latina chick named

Marcia, an Asian girl named Ling from the nail salon, and a girl named Keisha at the hair salon right next door. I learned fast that money could get me any girl I wanted and everything I wanted to buy. However, I wasn't locked up at Oakhill for selling drugs. Not this time. I was locked up for assault.

You see, I had been staying the night at my mom's crib since I'd been hustling in Capers until the wee hours of the morning. It was easier to crash at my mom's house since Grandma always put the latch on the door after midnight when I would miss curfew.

One night, while I was sleeping, I felt someone groping my family jewels. I opened my eyes halfway and saw my mom's new boyfriend Sheldon standing over me. He hurried out of the room when he saw me looking at him, and I went back to sleep. I wasn't sure if I was dreaming or not because I was tired. The next morning, I went downstairs to make sure I had everything before I headed home. Sheldon, who favored one of those curly-haired models on an *S-Curl* box was sitting at the dining room table eating a bowl of cereal. Mom was in the living room cussing somebody out on the phone. I grabbed my car keys off the dining room table and Sheldon winked his eye at me. That's when I knew he had really touched me in my sleep.

I went into the kitchen to the utility closet, and before Sheldon took his next bite, I hit him in the face with a metal shovel. Knocked him out cold.

"Lucci, what is wrong with you, boy?" Mom stood up abruptly, dropping the phone.

"He shouldn't have fondled me in my sleep," I said, standing over Sheldon as he slowly came to.

"Boy, Sheldon ain't touch you!" Mom yelled. "You're just jealous of our relationship."

She ran outside and waved down a police officer who happened to be patrolling the block. I tried to run, but when I tried to hop the fence outback, my pants got caught.

I've been at Oakhill for the past six months now for assault. Unfortunately, my dad was right, Mom and Turk never came to see me. My cousins visited often, including my homey Mitch. He was nice enough to move my Acura off the street and park it in Grandma's backyard. Mitch was a cool dude. He was Champ's best friend, and now I could see why.

Anyway, I was headed to see the psychiatrist, Mrs. Rogers. It was our last session together. Oakhill made you see a shrink when you got locked up. I had to see Mrs. Rogers once a week. She had diagnosed me with some kind of attention disorder with reckless behavior.

"Yo Lucci!"

My head jerked over my shoulder. It was TJ, an officer at the detention center with arms like Popeye and he wore a patch over one eye. He had muscles bigger than Hulk Hogan. Nobody messed with TJ.

"You got a phone call." TJ's voice boomed an echo down the hallway.

"Who is it?" I asked, pretending to scratch the back of my head as I hid a blunt behind my ear.

My homey Mook with the lazy eye had given it to me in the stairwell. Mook was from Potomac Gardens—a housing project down the street from my grandmother's house. He'd gotten locked up for carrying illegal firearms. Mook had looked out for me when guys from Sur Sum Corda housing projects tried to jump me when I first came here. Mook, and a guy named Peanut with a bumpy face, helped me to fight them off. Peanut lived on 15th Street. The three of us have been tight ever since.

"Do I look like your answering service?" TJ snarled. "Come and get the phone and find out for yourself."

I walked down the hall and followed him inside the administrator's office.

"Ten minutes is all you got," TJ said, sitting back behind the desk and crossing his big, tattooed arms. He kind of

71

reminded me of Mr. Clean with his bald head. I started to check my reflection.

"Hello?" I answered the phone.

"Yeah Shorty, you know who this is. I got your message. I'll send my driver to come pick you up when you get out next week. You remember him, right?"

The voice on the other end was Turk's. I didn't think he was ever going to call me back since I had paged him over a week ago. He was big time now. I heard he drove around in limousines with fly honeys and partied with celebrities.

"Yeah, I know who he is." I gritted my teeth upset he was just calling me back.

"Listen, you won't like this, but my lieutenant gave your corner to a new guy."

"Why?"

"Because he's smart. You're gonna be too hot when you get out. The rules are to lay low for ninety days, remember?"

I rolled my eyes behind the phone. I hated the idea of another guy making money on my corner, but I couldn't say too much about it with TJ staring in my face.

"Stay with your grandmother. My lieutenant will hit you up when he wants you back on the block, alright?"

"Sounds like I don't have a choice."

"You don't. I keep telling you to keep your head on a swivel."

"But it wasn't my fault this time."

"It never is. Just stay off the block and that's an order."

Turk hung up on me, and I tried to play it cool like he didn't.

"Yeah, a'ight. I'll talk to you later. What I say? I said I'll call you later." I hung up.

TJ shook his head and said, "You're an idiot. I know he hung up on you with your crazy self. Go on to your therapy session. You need it."

When I got to Mrs. Rogers's office there was a sign on the door indicating that she was with another patient, so I sat down in the chair outside of her office and waited. I wondered what I was going to do for three months of not making any money. I had splurged on so many clothes and sneakers for me and my girlfriends. I had every Sergio Tacchini sweatsuit in different colors, pristine white-on-white K-Swiss and Reebok Classics. I had big truck jewelry, including a nameplate chain that read LUCCI from Nationals Jewelry store in Georgetown. We feasted on filet mignon at Morton's Steakhouse. Man, I had it all! With Turk taking me off the corner, I needed to figure out other ways to make money. I started plotting out my next moves inside my head when Mrs. Rogers' office door swung open.

"Donovan, I'm ready to see you now," Mrs. Rogers called me into her office. I snapped out of my daydream and followed her inside. It always smelled like coffee cream mixed with her cheap smelling drugstore perfume.

"Sorry I was delayed," she said, sitting down in her La-Z-Boy chair next to a floor lamp by the window. Her red lipstick looked dry and clumpy, as if she had been talking to clients all morning and hadn't drunk any water.

"Don't sweat it." I flopped down on the plush sofa across from her.

"During our last session, you mentioned that Sheldon touched you in your sleep, but you said the judge didn't believe you since you lied in his courtroom about other things you had done in the past, correct?"

"Yep. He didn't believe me. He was sending all of us black boys to juvie while the white boys got community service."

"Well, you know what they say, 'don't do the crime if you can't do the time.' Maybe you should have called the police instead of hitting Sheldon with the shovel."

I smirked. "Easy for you to say, Mrs. Rogers. You never lived in a ghetto like me. That's how we handle things."

"Donovan, you can rise above your circumstances. There are many successful people who grew up poor."

73

I crossed my arms. "Like who?"

"John H. Johnson grew up poor," she mentioned.

I jerked my head back. "Who is that?"

"Don't you read *Ebony Magazine?* He's the founder. And then there is Maya Angelou, Oprah Winfrey, and the Reverend Jesse Jackson."

"Oh, I knew that." I waved her off, but I really didn't. I grabbed the stress ball off the table and started squeezing it.

"Anyway, even though the judge didn't believe you this time, I did. I take what happened to you very seriously," she said, pausing to jot down some notes on her clipboard. "I'm recommending that you not go back to your mother's house. It's not safe."

"Alright," I said, nonchalantly, tossing the ball up in the air and catching it before it hit the floor.

"Speaking of your mom, she's fallen off the wagon again. I was notified that the police picked her up this morning for shoplifting at Woodies downtown. That's another reason I'm not sending you back there. Your mother is sick and needs rehab again."

"I'm not surprised."

"The bigger question is, what are you going to do when you get out of here this time?"

"I don't know." I shrugged.

"A man without a plan will always return to his past," she said, and went into another lecture. I tuned her out and stared at the clock on the wall. I knew chow would be starting soon. We'd probably have beans with weenies again. Afterwards, we'd watch TV in the rec room. Although there was nothing thrilling about watching a small TV in a giant room that smelled like Pine-Sol, it was better than sitting here in therapy. Besides, I needed to talk to Mook and Peanut. We needed to come up with a plan to make some money once we got out.

"Donovan, are you listening to me?" Mrs. Rogers asked.

"What you say?"

"I was saying, this is our last session. Is there anything else I need to know?"

"Nope."

"Very well then," Mrs. Rogers quickly scribbled her signature at the bottom of some kind of form on her clipboard and slid it into my file underneath. "I do hope you stay out of trouble next time."

"I will."

She pouted a doubtful look. "I sure hope you're right this time."

CHAPTER 12
BABY, IT'S COLD OUTSIDE

RAVEN

Karyn White and Babyface were crooning "Love Saw It" from my boombox on my dresser as I rolled over and nestled my head into the fold of Taj's arm. My body still felt like it was on fire. I snaked my hand over his bare chest, looked up into his eyes and said, "Let's go another round."

"What?" Taj's eyelids twitched.

"You heard me."

"Three times is enough. Look, I gotta go." Taj moved his arm so quickly that my head plopped against the pillow.

"Fine!" I wrinkled the corner of my mouth and put on an offended pout.

"Besides, didn't you tell me that nerdy guy Adrian was coming over to tutor you in math today?"

"I forgot Adrian was coming over."

"I bet you did," Taj said, tugging his hoodie over his head. His corkscrew curls easily snapped back neatly in place. "Come and walk me to the door."

"You know how to get there on your own."

"So now you're gonna act salty?" He scrunched his face. "I'm getting tired of you acting like a brat when you can't have your way."

"What-*ever*." I stood up off the bed and crossed my arms. "Just put the bottom lock on when you leave."

Taj walked out of my room, huffing in frustration, but I didn't care. When I heard the door slam shut, I went and took a shower and started getting ready before Adrian came over. I blew my wet hair dry before the mirror and couldn't help but gaze at the picture of Taj smiling back at me. He was wearing his purple and white football uniform with the ball cupped in the fold of his arm. He kind of favored Champ, who I missed deeply. Champ would probably be playing basketball at Duke by now if he was still here. I weighed on what Taj meant by getting tired of me having my way as I brushed my hair into a ponytail.

I should be tired of him.

Taj had cheated on me twice, and each time I'd forgiven him and taken him back. Boogie and Leslie told me I deserved better, but who else can top Taj? He was the cutest guy in school. He was athletic and popular. All the girls wanted Taj, but he was mine.

But maybe it was time for me to explore other guys. I'm young. I will be sixteen soon, and I've only been with Taj. My friends on the cheerleading squad are already on their fourth and fifth boyfriends. Adrian could be my first adventure to the other side.

I snatched Taj's picture from the corner of my mirror and tossed it in my dresser drawer. Instead of getting dressed, I slipped on a sexy short pink nightgown from Victoria's Secret and sprayed my neck with Tommy Girl.

Ding-dong.

I looked out of my bedroom window and saw Adrian at the door. He was tall, long-legged, and skinny with a short fade haircut. He wore nice thin-framed glasses and played saxophone for our school band. Kind of dorky, but with a cute smile.

Our teacher, Mr. Shalini, paired Adrian as a tutor for me for trigonometry. Mr. Shalini gave me a D this term. He told my parents I would end up in summer school if I didn't bring up my grade.

"We pay too much money for you to be making Ds," my parents had said.

I never wanted to go to St. Francis High School in the first place. I was hoping since we moved from Clinton to Brandywine that Mom would let me attend a public school.

Maybe my classes wouldn't be so difficult, but no, they insisted I continue with my private school education.

"The standards are better," Mom had said.

Adrian must've sensed someone staring at him because he looked up. When he saw me in the window, he waved his hand enthusiastically and a big braces smile spread across his face. I was glad I no longer wore braces, but Adrian's were kind of cute. I took note of his fashion taste, too. He was wearing a blue and neon green Gore-Tex coat, a turtleneck sweater, blue jeans with peanut-butter-colored Timberland boots. Even his backpack matched his coat. I closed the curtains and hurried down the stairs.

I opened the door and pulled Adrian inside by the collar of his coat. Before he could say hello, I stood on my tiptoes and kissed him on the mouth.

"Right this way!" I pulled him by the hand and rushed him upstairs.

"Are your parent's home?" he yelped.

"Nope." I pushed him inside my room and shut the door. I took his backpack off his shoulder and tossed it across the room by my study desk.

"Have a seat." I tapped my hand on the bed next to me. Adrian eased down slowly with his eyes darting around the room.

"Are you sure it's okay for me to tutor you in here?" Adrian asked, tapping his boots against the floor.

"Hold on to this." I placed a condom pack in the middle of Adrian's sweaty palm. "When you're ready, slide it on. You know how to use it, right?" I puckered my brow.

"Uhm, shouldn't we talk first?" He gulped.

"I don't have time for that."

"Wha-wha-what about you and Taj?"

I pushed his shoulders back on the bed and straddled him.

"Don't worry about Taj. Let me take you to the moon," I whispered seductively in his ear as I unzipped his pants.

"Wait, what was that?"

"I didn't hear anything."

"I did. It came from downstairs."

I rolled off him and opened my bedroom door to listen. I heard keys unlocking the front door.

"Oh shoot, that's my mother. She's home early!"

"Oh no!" Adrian's eyebrows shot off like firecrackers.

"Quick, jump out the window!"

Adrian lifted the window and poked his head out. He took one look down at the snowy front yard and how far he would have to jump and said, "No way."

"Raven!" Mom called. I could hear her high heels climbing the marble staircase. She had purchased our new house when she became a partner for a personal injury law firm. She's helping Aunt Naomi and Uncle Henry file a civil suit against the drunk driver who killed Champ.

"Yes?" I shouted back, and simultaneously hissed for Adrian to help me set up the room like we'd been studying.

"Are you here by yourself? Whose car is that in our driveway?" she asked, her footsteps approaching my room.

I pulled a school T-shirt over my gown and stepped into a pair of shorts. I jumped on the bed in the nick of time and opened the textbook as Mom walked in. She was wearing a Donna Karen navy-blue pants suit with a white shirt. It was court day, and Mom always wore suits on court days.

"Hello." Adrian waved warily. "I'm Adrian Scott. I'm just tutoring Raven in trigonometry."

Mom shot Adrian a look that clearly said *get out*. But instead, she asked firmly, "What is he doing up here in your room?"

"He just told you he's tutoring me."

"Girl, don't you get smart with me. He can tutor you downstairs. And why is that window open as cold as it is outside?"

"It was hot in here." I walked over and shut it.

"I should go." Adrian stood up from my study desk chair.

"You do that and zip your fly on the way out." Mom pointed.

Adrian's face flushed red. He quickly zipped his pants and gathered his books.

"And Raven, are you wearing something underneath that T-shirt? I never knew that shirt was made with pink lace at the collar."

"I uhm...I was taking a nap before Adrian came over, and I forgot he was supposed to tutor me today, so I just threw this on right quick."

"Girl, you mean to tell me you couldn't think of a better lie than that? Do I look like boo-boo the fool?" Mom's voice shouted a few octaves higher than usual.

"Bye, Raven. See you at school tomorrow. Bye, Mrs. Brooks." Adrian waved, then he bumped into my dresser, practically stumbling out of the room.

"It's Ms. Walker." Mom rolled her eyes in dramatic fashion. "For your information, I am not married to Raven's father anymore."

"Oh, sorry. Goodbye, Ms. Walker." Adrian hurried out of the room and out of the house.

"Raven, get your father on the phone, right now," Mom demanded.

Oh boy, here we go with another lecture. What was Dad going to do? Leave his new wife Veronica and the twins, Raymond and Rayna, to come over here? I dialed my father, but I wasn't surprised he didn't pick up, so I left a message.

"I thought you were supposed to be going with Taj," Mom said.

"I am."

"Then why was Adrian up here?"

"I told you, but you didn't believe me."

Mom walked over, leaned down, and picked up the condom package that I didn't know had fallen on the floor at the foot of my bed.

"At least you got sense enough to use protection."

"I'm always careful. The last thing we need in this house is another lonely child."

"Girl, you get smart with me one more time and I'm going to knock your teeth down your throat."

By the time my dad called back, I was halfway to sleep. I overheard him and Mom arguing on the phone.

"...and Raven is too grown acting. You need to plan to spend more time with her. Girls need fathers too, you know? I don't care that you had to pick up the twins from daycare today. You should've taken Raven's call. What if it were an emergency?"

Mom still expected us to be a priority in Dad's life, regardless of his other obligations. I didn't want to hear anymore, so I pressed the pillows against my ears and forced myself to sleep.

The next day, Mom didn't speak to me when she came downstairs. I was sitting at the granite countertop in the kitchen, eating a bagel and fruit. She walked right past me, rolling her eyes. Our new house was a single-family home with all the bells and whistles that could fit in one of those modern home magazines, including a swimming pool out back. I guess she believed a new house would fix all that was wrong in our lives.

Mom made a pot of coffee while simultaneously talking on the cordless phone about work. She didn't even notice I was wearing her big hoop earrings. She was fussing at someone about not receiving discovery documents. When I finished eating, I dropped the plate in the sink and left without a goodbye. She probably didn't notice that either.

At School...

As I walked down the hall, my friends congregated at their lockers, talking, and laughing. Donna happened to look up and see me heading to my class.

"Hey Raven, guess what?" Donna, who was always perky, walked up to me and blocked my path.

"What?" I asked, unenthused.

"Sebastian asked me to the homecoming dance."

"So."

"So? You know that means we will all have a date now."

"Whoop-de-doo."

"Dang girl, what's wrong with you? Got your period or something?"

"Nope."

"Well, let's talk more at lunchtime. The bell just rang for first period." Donna hurried off to class.

I needed coffee even though I didn't drink it. My parents' arguing disturbed my rest, and I hoped I wasn't going to fall asleep as I headed to my history class. I spotted Taj down the hall, talking to Melissa next to her locker. She and I competed in a teen beauty pageant last summer, where we tied for first place. Taj and everyone else had agreed that it shouldn't have been a tie.

"Melissa's got nothing on you, babe," Taj had said, and yet he was standing with Melissa as she grabbed something from her locker.

Taj's back was toward me, but I recognized those bowlegs and broad shoulders anywhere. I walked past my history class and headed quietly in their direction. When I got close enough, I loudly cleared my throat.

"Guess I'll see you later, Taj." Melissa glared at me over Taj's shoulder, causing him to turn around.

Taj's inner eyebrows raised in surprise to see me.

"What was that all about?" I asked in a tone that was unconsciously like my mother's.

Taj's lips curved slightly. "Nothing," he said, and proceeded down the hall.

"Don't you walk away from me, boy."

Taj kept walking, and I ran up to him and stepped in front of him to block his path.

"What do you have to say for yourself, Taj Gregory?"

"Ms. Brooks, lower your voice and move on to class," the hall monitor, Mr. Karpinski, interrupted.

"Taj, answer me!" I shouted, ignoring Mr. Karpinski.

"You know what, I'm sick of you being a brat, Rave. Just leave me alone and go on to class."

"I'll go to class after you tell me why you were all up in Melissa's face."

"I said it was nothing, but maybe it should've been." Taj turned around and walked away, but I rushed up to him and pulled his arm.

"Get off me!" He snatched his arm back. "I'm tired of you. I don't want to deal with your childishness anymore. It's over." Taj threw up his hands.

"You can't break up with me!"

"I just did." Taj turned the corner and went to his class.

"Ms. Brooks, I said to—"

"—I'm going to class now, Mr. Karpinski." I rolled my eyes and stomped down the hall to history class.

I wanted to abandon myself to a dark room and never come out again. Instead, the history teacher subjected me to reading the next paragraph in our textbook about the rise of imperialism and colonialism. I read the texts with my lips quivering, holding back tears I didn't want anyone to see.

When the bell rang, I ran to the girls' room and cried in the stall. In the back of my mind, I could hear Champ's voice when he once told me that crying was for wimps. I wiped away my tears and tried not to be one.

After classes ended, Adrian and I met in the school library for tutoring. He kept apologizing about being in my bedroom.

"It's fine, Adrian. You don't have to keep apologizing," I said. "My mother trips out like that sometimes, don't sweat it, alright?" I dropped my books on the table as we sat down together.

"SHHHH." A girl in the corner tried to hush me.

"You shut up," I snapped.

"Raven, are you okay?" Adrian asked.

"I'm fine, but she's not going to shut me up."

"No offense, but this *is* a library."

"Look, Adrian, let's just get on with this, okay?"

"Okay." He glared at me with concern. "We're on the triple angle identities lesson, page fifty."

I riffled through the pages until I came across the lesson in the book.

"Are you sure you're okay?" Adrian's eyes softened behind his glasses.

I shook my head slowly and uttered a faint, "No."

"I heard about Taj breaking up with you for Melissa. That wasn't cool, the way he went about it."

"Taj is selfish. Nobody thinks about me. Not him, not my mother or my father, nobody."

"Do you want to get out of here? Like, go grab a burger or something?"

I sniffed and nodded my head yes.

We went to a burger spot down the street from our school, ordered two burger meals, and took a booth in the back. Adrian was doing most of the talking. I was busy trying to remember if I'd made my next hair appointment. Lately, I'd been wearing a style that was long and curly like Lark Voorhies on *Saved by the Bell*.

"Earth to Raven." Adrian snapped his fingers before my eyes.

I blinked. "Oh, sorry."

"I was asking if you liked your food because you barely touched anything."

I glanced down at the burger on the tray. I'd taken only a bite before pushing it aside.

"I guess I wasn't that hungry."

"I understand. If you want to talk about what happened with you and Taj, I'll listen."

"Really? Most boys don't want to hear about other guys."

"I'm not saying Taj is on my favorite person's list, but if it'll help you feel better, I'm all ears."

"You know, that's kind of you, but I don't want to talk about Taj right now."

"Fair enough." Adrian grabbed his soda and slurped whatever was left.

"Do you have a girlfriend?"

Adrian snorted. "Wow, that came from left field."

"Well?"

"We broke up. Why?"

"I'm just curious. You mind if I ask you a few rapid-fire questions?"

He leaned back, rubbed his chin hairs, and said, "Lay it on me."

"Just be yourself. Answer the questions honestly, okay?"

"Go ahead already."

"Okay. What do you do for fun?"

"Rock climbing, swimming, and playing my sax."

"Favorite color?"

"Blue like the ocean."

"Music?"

"Nirvana, Poison, and Guns N' Roses."

"One last question."

He leaned on his forearms and stared me directly in the eyes. "Shoot."

"Would you like to go out with my cousin Leslie?"

He frowned, eased his back against the booth. "No."

"Oh, come on!"

"I'm here with you."

I blushed. "I appreciate this lunch, but I'm not ready for another relationship right now."

"Who's asking?"

"Well, I'm just making sure we're on the same page."

"I'll take being your friend...for now."

Adrian pulled out his wallet and dropped a twenty-dollar bill on the table, as if paying for the lunch wasn't a big deal. Something about his mannerisms reminded me of my dad, and I liked that too. But I couldn't possibly be seen walking around school with him after Taj. I knew everyone would think I was with him on a rebound or settling for someone from a nerdy group. That wasn't my style. For now, we'll just kick it and see how things go.

CHAPTER 13
SWEATER WEATHER

LESLIE

I was in my bedroom working on my essays for my college applications. I'd applied to all out-of-state schools— Columbia, Temple, and Spelman. I was almost eighteen and ready to start a new life of my own. The journalism departments for each school had required a writing sample, but I couldn't think of what to write. My classmate, Kimberly Carter, who we all call KC, was sitting on my carpeted bedroom floor with her legs crossed. She was reading over her own college applications. We'd been studying together at my house every Wednesday after school.

I sat at my study desk, trying to think of what to write for my essays. I figured I would write about the Berlin Wall and how after twenty-eight years it finally came down last month in November, opening the West, but as I started to write about it, I felt stuck. It wasn't like I didn't feel for the people in Berlin who hadn't seen their families in years because of the wall, but I didn't live there. I couldn't relate to that type of experience. I balled up the piece of paper and tossed it across the room, and it hit the side of the trash can.

"Champ would've made that." I exhaled heavily through my nose in disappointment.

KC reached over and tossed the paper in the trash for me.

"Wait, that's it." I tapped my chin with my pointy finger.

"What's it?" KC asked with a perfectly arched eyebrow.

"I can write about Champ."

Champ was close to my heart, and I could easily write an essay about his impact on our family and our community. Not a day went by that I didn't think about Champ. People in our community talked about Champ as much as they did another phenomenal basketball player that we lost, Len Bias.

"Or you could write about your mother's muteness," KC suggested.

"I don't think it's my story to tell."

"Who else can tell your mother's story besides you?" she asked, removing her dark-framed reading glasses. They always gave her a career woman's look when she wore them.

"I don't want people to know my family's business. Besides, I don't know all the details."

"If you're going to be a journalist, don't you think it's time that you do your research?"

"My grandmother always said if you go looking for trouble, you will find it."

"And *my* grandmother used to say, if you shake the tree, the ripest apple will fall."

"Writing about Mama is not an option."

KC shrugged. "Suit yourself."

I stood up from my study desk. The thought of probing into what happened to Mama made me uneasy. I needed something to eat to quickly take my mind off the idea.

"Are you hungry? I cooked a whole pan of lasagna yesterday, and there's still some left, if you don't mind leftovers," I offered KC.

"I don't mind at all."

Grandma was on the phone in the living room when KC and I went down to the kitchen to warm up the leftover lasagna. By the sound of her conversation, it was Lucci, and he needed a ride.

"...well, I'm sorry Turk's friend's car broke down. I can't come and get you because I sprung my ankle on the ice outside, and I don't want Leslie driving in this inclement weather," Grandma was saying. "I can call and ask Mitch, since he has a truck that can handle the snowy roads."

KC and I sat down in the dining room to eat and started chatting about school. A few minutes later, the doorbell rang, and Grandma grabbed her cane and hobbled toward the front door with one healthy foot and a booted other one. She returned to the living room with Mitch walking behind her. He helped her to sit down in her favorite recliner by the window. The two of them began to have small talk, and I watched Grandma hand him money. I assumed it was to pay him to pick up Lucci.

"So, have you put in your order for our yearbook yet?" KC asked in between small bites of lasagna.

"Not yet, but I heard you won for Most Attractive," I said, stuffing my mouth with another forkful of lasagna.

"I'd rather I won for Most Likely to Succeed and Smartest Girl, like you did."

"Ugh, I don't think those senior superlatives are bragging rights. Besides, being smart has never gotten me a date or a boyfriend."

"I wouldn't worry about that if I were you."

"Well, I do. You've seen how the guys walk by me as if I'm not even there." I poked around my plate with my fork. "The only time they notice me is when I raise my hand to answer a question that they can't answer, and then they sneer, 'know it all.'"

"Being attractive can be hard sometimes too, you know," KC confessed.

My eyes traced over her beautifully fitted striped turtleneck and leather skirt that accentuated her every curve. I only wished I had a body like hers. Raven said my style has always been a bit frumpy. Perhaps she's right.

I sipped my soda and said, "I see nothing *hard* about being pretty like you."

"Thank you, but if I had a choice, I'd rather a guy be interested in who I am as a person than how I look." KC bit a small piece of lasagna and chewed it slowly as if she was counting each chew before she swallowed.

"It's easy for you to say that, KC. You get all the cute guys."

"Most of them are bammas for real. Either they got peanuts for brains or only want to have sex, and even that isn't so great with those pretty boys since we're being honest."

"Whatever you say." I stuffed my mouth until my cheeks were filled like a chipmunk.

"By the way, you really shouldn't put so much food in your mouth at one time. My mother says that attraction is often how we carry ourselves."

"Oh." I held my hand over my mouth, feeling a little embarrassed.

"Hey Leslie." Mitch walked into the dining room, ducking his head under Grandma's grape ivy plant that hung on a hook.

I waved since my mouth was full.

"You want to ride with me to scoop up Lucci?" he asked.

His hair was a pool of shiny waves. By the look of his shapeup, neat mustache, and goatee, I could tell he'd just gotten a fresh cut. He was becoming more and more handsome the older he got.

I quickly swallowed my food and replied, "Sure, would you mind dropping my friend KC off at home first?"

"No problem. I'll be outside warming up my truck."

He blushed a handsome smile and put on his hat. His dark lashes draped his soft brown eyes like a teddy bear. They were the perfect complement to his evenly curved eyebrows. As he walked away, he had so much swagger in his walk that he could command a room.

"Wow, he's cute!" KC said, looking over her shoulder. Her back was facing the living room, so she didn't pay much attention to Mitch when he came in. "I've never seen him before. Does he go to Eastern?"

Back off girl. I wiped my mouth with a napkin.

"Mitch graduated two years ago."

"Oh, so he's a college guy now?"

"He works at the Safeway down the street," I said.

"I'll take an honest working guy any day."

I tilted my head. "A moment ago, you were tired of cute guys."

"Guys our age are immature, but Mitch may be a different story."

"Anyway, I'm going to take Mama dinner before we go. I'll bring your backpack and purse when I come back down."

"I can get my own things. Besides, I've always wanted to meet your mother." KC's cheeks rose with eagerness.

"I don't want you to be scared if she stares at you."

"I won't be."

Mama was sitting on the edge of her bed watching *Mr. Bean* when KC and I walked into her room. I set up her dinner plate on the TV stand and placed it in front of her. Her eyes were sparkling, and her lips curved in the corners, which meant she was in a happy mood. I just wished she would talk. I had been imagining, dreaming, hoping, and praying for her to utter at least one word. Mama still hasn't spoken a word, and I will be eighteen in a few months.

"Mama, this is my friend KC. We take English and chemistry classes together at Eastern." But Mama kept watching *Mr. Bean* as if KC wasn't there. I got upset because it was embarrassing to see Mama staring at the TV like KC was invisible.

"It's impolite not to at least look at the person you're being introduced to," I said to Mama, and turned the TV off. She dropped her chin and stared at the floor.

"It's okay, Leslie. Don't force her to do what she hasn't been doing." KC stepped in closer and extended her hand. "Hello, Ms. Walker. I'm Kimberly Carter, everyone calls me KC."

Mama slowly lifted her eyes and gave KC the once over. She started twiddling her thumbs and rocking back and forth, which meant she was nervous.

"Would you like for me to feed you your dinner?" KC offered.

"She knows how to eat it herself. She's not immobile," I snapped. "Her limbs work, and she knows how to do most things on her own. It's just that her mouth doesn't work."

"I see. Well, I'll go grab my things from your room. After all, that fine Mitch is waiting for us." She looked over her shoulder and winked back at me. She sounded a little too excited for Mitch, and I didn't like that.

I turned Mama's TV back on.

"I'm sorry, Mama. I didn't mean to get upset with you. It's just a little embarrassing that you can't talk." I leaned down and kissed her cheek.

Mama slowly raised her eyes and looked directly at me. It looked like she accepted my apology because her eyes softened, and she turned to eating her food and watching *Mr. Bean*.

KC and I climbed into Mitch's black Pathfinder. I sat up front and KC sat in the back. A Tribe Called Quest's song "Bonita Applebaum" was thumping from the CD deck, but his stereo system had way too much bass and made the windows rattle.

"Do you mind if I turn this down a little?" I shouted over the music.

"Not at all." Mitch shrugged.

We hadn't talked much over the past few years. He would occasionally do favors for Grandma like cut the grass or shovel snow, but Mitch seemed more distant after Champ died. We'd say hello to each other, but there wasn't much small talk between us. I always wondered if he remembered when he had kissed me. I know I will never forget about it.

"So, how have you been doing, Big Mama?" Mitch asked casually.

I knew he meant no harm by calling me "Big Mama," but I wished he hadn't. It was a reminder that I was still carrying around too much weight. I weighed 165 pounds.

My doctor had said, "All you need to lose is forty pounds and you'd be within your normal weight range." He made it sound as if I could click my heels three times and voila.

"I've been OK, I guess."

"So, what grade are you in now?" Mitch asked, in a tone like he was one of my elders. He was only twenty, not even the legal age to drink yet.

I started to say, *third grade.*

"I'm a senior." I put a little heaviness in my voice.

"Aw shucks. I bet you got a boyfriend now, don't you?"

"No, I don't."

"I told Leslie she's a sweet person. She'll find the right guy for her soon enough," KC emitted from the backseat.

"She sure will." Mitch chuckled and playfully hit my thigh.

"I haven't seen you around much these days," I mention, skipping the subject.

"Yeah, well, I been working a lot because my fiancée and I are expecting our first child."

Suddenly, my throat closed, and my tongue stuck to the roof of my mouth. I'd seen Mitch with a Latina girl a few times, but I didn't think it was that serious.

"Congratulations," KC said.

"Thanks. She's due in six months," Mitch responded proudly, glancing at KC in the rearview mirror.

I forced a swallow as my mind and heart raced with mixed emotions. In the back of my mind, I always felt Mitch and I would circle back to each other's hearts.

"Are you even sure you're ready to be a father?" I asked, but as soon as I did, I wanted to take it back. I couldn't hide my jealousy, wishing it was Mitch's baby inside my belly.

"Ready or not, the baby is still coming, and we're not going to adopt it, that's for sure," Mitch replied. "KC, am I headed in the right direction of where you live?"

KC craned her neck between the two seats up front. "Yes, keep straight, then make a right. I live by the Boys and Girls

Club on Mass Avenue." She pointed and eased back into her seat.

"Really? Do you know my fiancée, Angel? She lives on Massachusetts Avenue, too."

"She's the oldest Gonzalez sister, right?" KC asked.

"Yep, she has two younger sisters, Marcia and Lisa?"

"That's them, alright. They just moved here from California two years ago." KC gave him a suspicious grin.

"Why did you say it like that?" Mitch's brows pinched inward with concern.

"I don't want to cause any trouble, but guys are always running in and out of their house late at night when their mother is at work."

"Probably her sisters' boyfriends," Mitch said.

"Maybe you're right. Anyway, my house is the yellow one on the left." KC pointed, and Mitch pulled up to her house.

"See you at school tomorrow, Leslie."

"Bye."

The rest of the ride to pick up Lucci was Mitch asking me what was wrong. I told him nothing, but I was still processing the news of him being engaged and about to have a baby. Perhaps all of this was a sign for me to let go of my feelings for him once and for all. Raven seemed to have moved on from having a crush on him after all these years. Maybe it's time I did the same.

CHAPTER 14
A HAZY SHADE OF WINTER

MITCH

Anxiety kept me up all night. I crawled out of bed the next morning, noticing my clock read 6:05AM. I preferred to sleep in on my off days, but I was worried about what KC said yesterday.

I had tried to call Angel, but the phone line was busy all night. Figured her sisters had the line tied up. I thought of calling this morning, but Angel and the baby need their sleep. The rain had washed the remnants of snow away. I might drive over there this morning.

I happened to look up, and from across the street, Irene Walker was staring at me with her dark, smoldering eyes as if there was someone standing behind me. I waved my hand to say hello, and she just gazed at me. She really wasn't a bad-looking woman. She and Leslie had the same penny colored complexion with a golden undertone, but it was her eyes that told you something was off about her. I turned away from the window when my mother knocked on my bedroom door.

"Mitch," Mom called. "Can I come in?"

"It's open." I grabbed my pack of Newport and the ashtray from my dresser.

"Good morning, you're up early," Mom greeted me perkily. Her soft blue eyes always looked brighter in the morning.

"I couldn't sleep," I said, as the cigarette dangled from the corner of my mouth.

"Do you have to work today?" she asked, sipping coffee

from her thermos that had *The Georgetown University* scripted on the front. She was always a proud GT alum. I leaned my six-foot-two body against the window frame. Even in her nurse's uniform shoes, Mom stood five four. I towered over her like a giant.

"Nope, I'm off today since I been pulling double shifts these past two weeks." I turned my head so I wouldn't blow smoke her way. "The extra cash at Safeway will help me and Angel get our own apartment."

"I'm proud of you for working so hard, but you don't need to rush to move out." The caramelized nutty aroma from her thermos filled the air in the room and masked the tobacco smell. "You guys can live here awhile and save money."

"I need to take care of my own family. Once I become a Store Manager, we'll have enough to buy a house."

"Are you kidding?" Mom chuckled sarcastically. "Diapers alone will take most of your paycheck."

"Then I'll get a part-time job. We'll make it work."

"I just want what's best for you guys. You know, my coworker's son went into the military. He learned electrical engineering, and he's doing well for himself. Maybe you could join."

"And leave my family the way John left us?" I scoffed.

"You can take your family with you after bootcamp."

"I'm not going to be a deadbeat father like John."

Mom heaved a sigh. "Let's not go there this morning, okay?"

I bellowed out a halo of smoke above my head, and griped, "Yeah, OK."

"And quit smoking these cancer sticks." She snatched the cigarette from my lips and snuffed it out in the ashtray. "The baby can't live around this smoke, and neither can I."

"I'm working on quitting."

"Good. So, what are Angel's plans after she has the baby?"

"What do you mean?" I asked curiously.

95

"She's twenty-two. Shouldn't she be in school or working to help support the baby, too?"

"No. I don't want my wife to work. Her job will be to stay home and take care of the baby."

Mom propped her hand on her hip and shook her head. When she bit down on her bottom lip, I knew she was trying to avoid saying anything more.

"By the way, Bernard called you last night, but you were asleep."

"I just saw Bernard the other night. I'll call him soon. I like to take things slow."

She sipped her coffee slowly but a bit louder. I guess she was trying to make a point. I happened to like Bernard. He was a heart surgeon like Ben Carson. He always treated Mom nicely.

"Oh my, look at the time." Mom glanced at her watch. "I need to get going."

I followed her downstairs and walked her to the door.

"There are leftovers in the fridge if you get hungry." She grabbed her coat off the coatrack by the door. "And I know you're off today, but don't forget to call Dr. Shaw and tell him you need a refill on your medicine. I noticed the bottle on your dresser was empty."

"Ma...I don't need those things anymore."

"Honey, we've been down this road before and—"

"I haven't taken it in over a month now. I been throwing them in the trash."

"Mitch," she squawked. "You know you can't stop that medication abruptly. It could lead to suicidal thoughts."

"I know. I stopped them gradually. I feel fine." I shrugged.

"We'll talk about this later." She hurried out the door and down the front steps to her Toyota Celica.

"Yo, what's up, Mitch!" Lucci waved from across the street as I stood in the entryway.

He was connecting jumper cables to his Acura and his grandmother's Oldsmobile. When he started up his car, it sounded like a death howl. I think it had been sitting for too long since he had been locked up for the past six months. I figured he could use my help.

"What's up Lucci! Give me a second, I'll help you out," I shouted across the street, then shut the door, went upstairs, and got dressed.

When I came outside, Lucci and I connected the cables to my truck, but his car still wouldn't start.

"I don't understand how I was able to move the car from my grandmother's backyard to out front," Lucci shook his head.

"Maybe the battery died," I said.

Leslie peeked her head out the door. "Are you almost ready? I have an eight o'clock SAT prep class."

"Nah, my car won't start. I guess we'll have to walk," he replied.

"I can drop you guys off at school," I offered. "Besides, I need to swing by and see my girl Angel anyway."

"Angel?" Lucci shuddered. "Angel Gonzalez?"

"Yeah, you know her?"

"That's my girl Marcia's sister. Well, she's just one of my girls." He laughed.

"I see you, player player," I chuckled. I had tossed out my little black phone book when things got serious between me and Angel six months after dating.

"You can't take them Gonzalez girls seriously, dawg."

"We're engaged. That's serious to me," I said. We'd been dating a whole year now. Angel was perfect for me.

"Man, I can't believe you asked a freak to marry you."

"Hey, slow your road, my homey."

Lucci threw up his hands. "Hey man, I'm just calling it like I see it. What N.W.A say? You can't love these—."

"Shut up man, get your peanut head in the truck!" I cut him off and hit him playfully on the back of the head.

"Thanks for offering us a ride, Mitch." Leslie climbed up front.

After I dropped Leslie and Lucci off at school, I decided

to pay Angel a visit. Besides, we needed to discuss our wedding plans. We hadn't gone over any details as to whether we were getting married at the courthouse or a church. We hadn't even talked about baby names because I'd been busy working. I figured if it's a boy, he would be Mitch Jr., that's easy, but I have no idea what to name it if it's a girl.

It grew colder as I stood outside of Angel's door, waiting for her to answer. I waited a few more minutes, but when no one came to the door, I left. As I headed home, something in my gut told me to circle back around the block and try again. Perhaps it was all the talk from Lucci and KC that had me concerned.

When I circled the block and turned back onto Angel's street, my heart dropped to my feet. I spotted her kissing a dude with a high-top fade, wearing a red and blue Washington Bullets Starter jacket. Her mother worked at night, so I figured this dude stayed over with her, and she was letting him out before her mom came home.

My initial shock boiled into a rage when I saw him squeezing Angel's butt when he kissed her again. I slammed my foot on the brake to stop the truck, put the gear in park, and jumped out.

"Mitch, what are you doing here?" Angel's voice shook in surprise to see me as I walked up to her front porch.

High-top fade had his back toward me, but as soon as he looked over his shoulder, I punched him right in the face, knocking him over the handrail. He landed in the front yard. I was about to finish him off, but he caught his balance and took off running to his car.

"You shouldn't have done that!" Angel stomped back into the house and tried to close the door in my face, but I pushed it open. She had the audacity to wear the pink bathrobe and fuzzy slippers that I had bought her last Valentine's Day.

"Give me my ring back!"

"No, this is mine!" she shouted in her Spanish accent. I used to love it, but now, I hated it.

"I said give it back." I grabbed her left hand and twisted her wrist.

"Ow, you're hurting me."

"Leave my sister alone!" Marcia came rushing down the stairs with a tall, dark-skinned dude trailing behind her zipping up his pants.

I twisted Angel's hand and yanked the ring off her finger. She winced in pain.

"You're a loser, anyway. I hate you!" Angel shoved me.

"Knock it off!" I warned her with a pointy finger. "You're lucky I don't hit women, especially pregnant ones."

"There's no baby, stupid."

"What?"

"You heard me. You fell for the oldest trick in the book."

"So, wait...you were never pregnant?"

"No, I take the pill. I'm not stupid."

"Dang slim, you got played." The tall, dark-skinned dude shook his head.

"Big dummy," Marcia laughed.

"Lucci was right about y'all. You're both freaks, and I hope y'all die of AIDS."

"You're just jealous you weren't the only one," Angel slung her long hair over her shoulder and slightly poked her lips.

I got so angry that I grabbed her mother's vase and threw it toward her to scare her, but not hit her. It smashed against the wall and shattered into a thousand pieces. I stormed out of the door with Angel yelling behind me, "You're going to pay for that!"

I hopped in my truck and sped off. It was better for me to leave before things got out of control. At least, that's what I'd learned in my past therapy sessions.

I sped off in my truck, and kept telling myself, "Just breathe Mitch, count to ten. Take deep breaths. Easy boy...take it easy..."

My pounding heart started to slow as I made myself focus on the road. I came to a red light and watched a mother holding her child's hand while pushing another in a stroller. They were headed toward Payne Elementary School. Several children of all shapes and sizes laughed innocently as a crossing guard smiled and ushered them safely across the street. I imagined one of them could have been my future child, but it was all a lie.

I lost it and burst into tears. I needed my medicine. I needed to talk to Dr. Shaw. At that moment, I felt like hurting myself just to take the pain away.

CHAPTER 15
RED BOOTS

BOOGIE

Holidays were always the hardest to deal with since Champ had been gone. As annoying as it was, I missed waking up to Champ bouncing the basketball against the wall or talking to some girl late hours in the night when he was supposed to be sleeping. The other side of my room was as empty as my heart felt. Champ's twin bed used to be against the wall on the other side of the room. It's been replaced with a study desk. There used to be early mornings when Champ would wake me up to time his shooting in the driveway, using a stopwatch. He'd eventually shoot up to 50 shots in a minute. My brother was that good. He was also my hero at times, especially against bullies.

"Which one of you is Spike?" Champ had questioned the guys at my school playground when I was in the third grade.

Everyone stepped aside and pointed out Spike, who had busted my lip and called me the "F" word for playing Double Dutch with the girls. Spike was the same size as Champ and had stayed back a few times. Champ taught Spike a lesson that day and beat him up. I never had problems with Spike again.

"Listen, Boogie." Champ draped his long arm across my shoulders as we walked home that day. "I know I pick on you a lot, but I'm trying to toughen you up and prepare you for the cruel world out there, know what I'm saying?"

"I know."

"You have to start fighting back so people won't bully

you just because you're queer or because you happen to be smaller than they are."

"Alright."

"Promise?" Champ had puckered his brow.

"I promise. I will always fight back, even against you." I playfully punched him and took off running. He chased me home, but it was all in fun.

Our lives had been very different with Champ gone. Dad was battling with alcohol and arguing with Mom a lot. It was embarrassing to board the school bus in the mornings and see my father staggering along the sidewalk, drunk and singing loud tunes through slurred speech.

"Isn't that your father?" The students would point and laugh. I'd look away in shame.

Dad's job kept sending him to rehab and giving him warnings. Now he's on his last strike after crashing his truck into a light pole.

I tried to step into my brother's shoes by joining the basketball team at a recreation center near my house, but I wasn't as good as Champ. After turning over the ball several times and shooting one too many airballs, Dad stopped coming to my games. And when I'd try to make conversation with Dad and debate the basketball games on TV, he would belt out an annoying grunt and say, "Pass the peanuts."

Eventually, I gave up on sports. My real passion was dance. I wanted to be a backup dancer like I'd seen in music videos. When I asked my mother about taking hip-hop dance classes, she said, "It's fine with me, but check with your father to make sure he's okay with it too."

"Dancing is for sissies," Dad snarled, without even looking up from the Sunday paper.

I chided, "Michael Jackson never felt that way."

Dad lowered the paper just enough for me to see his big dark eyes. "Well, you're not Michael Jackson."

Obviously, I wasn't the apple of my father's eye, but my sister Jasmine, now three, was Dad's pride and joy. After my mom gave birth to Jasmine, dad sobered up for a few months, but everything quickly changed after the vehicular manslaughter trial involving my brother.

"Are you freaking kidding me?" Dad blurted out angrily in the courtroom that day. "That racist murdered my son with his truck and you're only sentencing him to three years?"

"Order in the court!" The judge, who was an older White man, whacked his gavel on the desk. Dad continued to shout at the judge and yell obscenities until the judge lost his patience.

"Mr. Walker, I'm sentencing you to twenty-four hours in jail to cool off, and there will be more time for you if you don't calm down. Bailiff, remove Mr. Walker from the courtroom immediately."

Two officers grabbed my father and cuffed him. Dad left the courtroom shouting, "I want justice for my son!"

Unfortunately, Dad's sobriety went out the window after that day in court. He keeps relapsing. It's been six months since his last drink, and this is the longest he's been sober. We'll see if it lasts.

Speaking of court stuff, my Aunt Diane has been helping my mom and dad with their civil suit over Champ's death. It turns out that the truck belonged to a company called Maynard Billard Construction. Mr. Duckworth worked for them. Aunt Diane said Maynard Billard is one of the largest construction companies in our area. They're suing for negligence. I sure hope they win.

Today was Christmas, and I slept in late. With Champ gone, there was no reason for me to hurry downstairs to open my gifts. Besides, I was almost fifteen and not a freaking kid anymore. Christmas was for kids like my sister Jasmine.

Anyway, I went downstairs to the living room, and honey, let me tell you, I thought Toys "R" Us had marched in and performed a parade. Toys were scattered everywhere. The Temptations were crooning "Silent Night" from the stereo in the corner, and Mom was setting up Jasmine's little dollhouse in the opposite corner. Dad sat on the floor with Jasmine, tickling her with her new Furby stuffed animals. I wondered what my parents were going to buy Jasmine by the time she was sixteen. A Porsche? This child had way too many toys.

"Well, hello." Mom stepped away from the doll house and gave me a hug and kiss. "Your gifts are over there in the chair."

She pointed to the round-back chair next to the fireplace, as she sat back down crisscross style on the floor and continued to place miniature furniture pieces inside the dollhouse.

I could tell by the gift tag inscription—NOLAN written in all caps—that they were gifts from my dad. The first box I opened had two pairs of blue denim jeans inside. The next box had two plain long-sleeved oxford shirts—one white and the other plaid, and the last box had two packs of brief underwear. I was not about that brief life. I liked boxers so I could feel free. I knew I would have to redesign the clothes my father bought me to make them fashionable for the 90s. Otherwise, I'd look like a scarecrow in the middle of a cornfield. In my mind, I knew I could cut the pants at the knees to make them look like the Used jeans brand. As for the plaid shirt, I figured I could rip the sleeves off, pop the collar up, and wear it like a vest over the white oxford shirt. All hope wasn't lost with the farmer-type of clothes, I guess.

Dad noticed the contemplative look on my face as I strategized my fashion plans. He looked up from the floor and asked, "What are you waiting for? Try them on and make sure they fit."

"I will do it later," I said, setting the clothes aside on the arm of the chair. I grabbed the last box. It was from my mother. The gift tag read "Boogie." My lips curved a smile in anticipation. I quickly tore the gift wrap off the box and opened the lid. Inside the box was a pair of red suede Timberland boots.

"Aw, thanks Mom." I smiled. "These are so *ka-ute!*"

"I saw how you were gawking at them on display at Up Against the Wall last week."

She smiled back. She was the queen who always saved my day. I was going to rock the red boots with a matching red blazer, a denim blue shirt with a red bowtie, and the pair of blue denim jeans that Dad had bought me. I also had a red baseball cap upstairs that I could use as an accessory with the outfit. My look was going to be preppy.

My dad quickly stood up from the floor, grunting and complaining that his knees had stiffened up from playing with Jasmine. He stood in front of me with his protruding beer belly, shook his head, and pointed.

"What the heck are those?"

I clucked my tongue. "Boots."

He shot a bulldoggish frown in Mom's direction. "Naomi, why would you buy him *red* boots? He's not a girl."

"Oh honey, relax. You know Boogie likes to dress different from everyone else."

"No son of mine is wearing red boots!" Dad snatched the box out of my hands and stormed out of the house. Immediately, we heard two loud thumps and knew he'd thrown the boots in the trash can by the driveway.

"Why? Just why would he do that?" I flipped my hands as I jerked up from the chair, and stomped as I went back up the steps.

Henry Walker Sr. was a mood killer if I ever seen one. I was getting sick and tired of him holding out a ruler and expecting me to measure up to his rigid standards. What was so wrong with me wearing red boots? No other guy in school wore red Timberlands. I would be the first and I would be unique. Being like everyone else was boring. I wanted to stand out. Why was that so hard for my dad to see? I'm going to fix him. He needs to learn to accept me for who I am. I went into my room, slammed the door, and didn't come out until it was time for us to go to Grandma's house for Christmas dinner.

CHAPTER 16
SNOW ANGELS

RAVEN

Mom's Audi inched slowly through the snow on the streets as she pulled up in front of Grandma's three-story house with its white vinyl siding, black paneled framing around the windows, and brick steps painted with several coats of gray. We'd been hoping for a white Christmas, and we got it.

I was happy that Mom and I celebrated Christmas together this morning without Gerald. He'd flown back to Boston to visit his family since he had spent Thanksgiving with us. Gerald was an attorney like Mom, except he practiced criminal law. I overheard Mom telling one of her friends on the phone that Gerald had just turned fifty-eight. I think he's too old for my mother, who is only forty-one. He was probably graduating from high school when she was just born. I hoped Gerald's visit back home in Boston would last for a long time. It was fun having my mother all to myself this winter break. We'd gone shopping together, cooked, and she took my cousins and I snowtubing in West Virginia. I couldn't wait to see what she had in mind for New Year's.

After Mom parked the car, I stepped out onto the pavement one leather boot at a time and tried to balance myself carefully on the snowy, icy ground. The crisp cold air bit into my cheeks, so I tightened my scarf around my neck and made sure my long black leather trench was buttoned all the way down. Lucci and his friends, Mook and Peanut, threw snowballs at each other in the middle of the street.

Seeing them gave me an eerie feeling and reminded me of when Champ died. I tried to ignore the passing thought as I helped Mom retrieve our prepared dishes from the trunk of the car.

"Yo Raven, think fast!" Lucci shouted.

As soon as I turned around, a snowball smacked me in the face. My flesh immediately reacted with pain that throbbed from the bridge of my nose to my mouth. I tried to run after him, but my feet skidded against the icy pavement, and before I could catch my balance, I fell flat on my face in the snow. The guys all burst into a belly-gut of laughter. I'd just gotten my hair done and had made up my face with cute makeup.

"Raven, are you OK?" Mom took hold of my hand and pulled me up from the ground as snowy crystals slid down my leather pants.

"I'm fine!" I grunted, feeling the heat of embarrassment in my face. Mom's cheeks puffed with air as she tried to hold in her laugh.

"It's not funny, Mom!"

"I'm sorry, kiddo, but that was hilarious."

Family and friends filled Grandma's house. She greeted everyone from her favorite recliner, while simultaneously watching the Washington Redskins play the Dallas Cowboys on her brand-new TV. Mom and I smiled as we walked by. My mother had bought the forty-inch TV for Grandma as an early Christmas present from Circuit City. She looked happy that Grandma seemed to be enjoying it better than the one she'd gotten from Fingerhut. She and my great aunts and uncles cheered loudly as their favorite team scored a touchdown.

"Leslie, be sure to fix your mama a plate too!" Grandma hollered from the living room. A few smaller children ran past her, chasing each other with their new toys in hand.

In the kitchen, there was already a smorgasbord of food on the kitchen countertops. We had everything. Mac 'n' cheese, deviled eggs, honey ham, a variety of chicken cooked different ways, turkey, yams, cranberry sauce, stuffing, collard greens, potato salad, you name it. We really didn't need any more food, but Mom didn't believe in showing up empty-handed. She and I had made a cabbage, a seafood salad, and baked trays of brownies.

Leslie made at least seven different plates and almost dropped them as she headed back to the living room.

"Who are all these plates for?" I stepped forward to help free her hands.

"Our elders who are in the living room watching the game," she said. "You know Aunt Sarah has a bad knee, and Uncle James had his hip replaced. Besides that, I couldn't just take plates to them and not anyone else. Their grandchildren need to eat, too."

"You shouldn't have to do all of this yourself."

"Raven is right. Do you want me to call Lucci inside to help you out?" Mom asked.

"That's okay, Aunt Diane. Oops, I forgot about the dinner rolls." Leslie opened the oven. Her eyes drooped with exhaustion as she removed the dinner rolls and started to butter them.

"Raven, I'll take the plates in the living room. You take your Aunt Irene her dinner," Mom said.

"Okay."

"Thank you, guys, for your help. I need to set the dining room table so the rest of us can sit down and eat soon," Leslie said, and she took the dinner rolls to the six-seated dining-room table. There were so many in my family that we always ate in intervals.

I went upstairs to Aunt Irene's room, knocked on the door, and peeped my head inside. When I was younger, I used to be scared of Aunt Irene and the way she would stare out in space, but now I feel sorry for her. I wished she could talk and be normal like everyone else.

"Hi Aunt Irene, I brought you some dinner."

She was standing at her window, and when I stood by her to see what she was looking at, I saw Lucci and his friends. They weren't throwing snowballs at each other anymore, but they were sitting on the receding wall smoking blunts and drinking beer.

"They're always up to no good, aren't they?" I shook my head and turned from the window. I noticed Aunt Irene was wearing a cute red sweater with Santa Claus on the front, blue jeans, and cute red leather boots as if she was going somewhere, but she wasn't. Maybe Leslie had her dress that way in case she wanted to come downstairs or if family came up to visit with her.

"Would you like me to set it on your food tray stand?" I asked, but of course Aunt Irene didn't answer. She didn't even look at me to acknowledge that I was in the room.

A spotless room, I might add. It was very clean, with vacuum lines running throughout the carpet, and it smelled like citrus potpourri. Leslie always kept the house clean, but her mother's room was immaculate. I didn't even see a wrinkle on the floral bed sheets. Leslie probably ironed the wrinkles out.

I set Aunt Irene's dinner tray at the foot of her bed where she liked to sit and watch TV. As I moved throughout her room, I caught a glimpse of myself in the mirror on her dresser next to her bed. I needed to touch up my makeup. I walked over to the mirror and examined myself closer, fluffing out my hair with my hand.

I spotted an old Polaroid picture of Aunt Irene tucked in the corner of the mirror. She wore bell-bottom blue jeans with a halter top and a big Afro. She was smiling as she sat on the grass surrounded by books, and her back leaned against a tree. I could see that Leslie favored her a lot, the way her cheeks almost touched her eyes when she smiled.

The photo looked like it may have been taken on Howard's campus. The founder's library clock was in the background. As I looked closer, I noticed the shadow of a man taking the picture. I wondered if he was the same guy she and my mom had fought over. My mom said she was really hurt when Aunt Irene took him from her. I think she said his name was Evan. I couldn't imagine Aunt Irene being a spiteful person, especially since everyone in the family always said she was kind to everyone. And if Leslie is just like her mom in personality, I'm sure Aunt Irene meant no harm.

I pulled out my makeup kit so I could reapply my makeup. I could see Aunt Irene through the mirror. She turned on her TV and sat down to eat.

"Hey girl!"

Boogie entered the room, and I glanced at him over my shoulder.

"Hey Cuz, I don't remember seeing you downstairs. What's in the bag? A gift for me?"

"We just got here. No, this isn't a gift for you," he said, then greeted Aunt Irene and kissed her cheek. Her lips curved into a slight smile. It made my heart feel glad that she knew we cared about her.

"So, whose gift is in the bag if it isn't mine?" I asked again, staring at him behind me in the mirror.

"You're so nosy. I have something in here I need to change into."

"Is it a dress?" I laughed.

"Not this time," he chuckled as he walked over and stood next to me. "So, how does the makeup feel on your face?"

"It makes me feel glamorous."

"Well, you're a diva honey. You look beautiful with or without makeup."

I gave him a playful punch. "Aw, thanks Cuzzo."

"Raven!" my mom called from downstairs. "Your father is here."

"Oh great!" I rushed out of the room and down the stairs.

My father stood by the front door looking tall and handsome in his fur hooded flight bomber jacket, blue jeans, and black boots.

"Hey Pumpkin." Dad squeezed me in his arms. His cologne always smelled like soft sandalwood.

"I'm so happy to see you, Dad. I didn't know you were coming over here."

"Well, I can't stay long."

"Why not?"

"Veronica and I have a flight to catch. We're headed to Aspen for a little vacation while her folks are keeping the twins."

"Funny, we never did make it to Aspen to go skiing." Mom crossed her arms and tightened her lips.

"I don't recall that being all my fault, Diane. You had bought that expensive land that your new house sits on now without discussing it with me," Dad shifted his eyes from Mom back to me. "Anyway, I was not going to leave town without making sure you received your gift. Follow me outside."

I grabbed my coat, and Mom grabbed hers. She had to be nosy. As soon as we stepped outside, I saw a brand-new white Mercedes convertible double-parked out front with a red ribbon on the hood.

"You bought me a car?" My jaw dropped.

"Veronica helped me pick it out for you."

"Make sure Veronica reminds you about my child support check that's due January first."

"I know that, Diane." Dad tightened his jaw and shook his head.

Veronica stepped out of the driver's seat, one long, bony leg at a time. She wore a short leather skirt with a mink coat. She'd dyed her dark hair blonde, and it was styled in big curls. A big goofy smile came across her face as she handed me the car key.

"Merry Christmas, Raven." Veronica hugged me. My internal parts were screaming *get your hands off me*. But my mouth forced a smile.

"You too," I said reluctantly.

Veronica always tried too hard to be like my mother, but she went overboard. She wore enough makeup that could put a clown to shame, but she probably thought it made her look prettier than my mom. And she couldn't accept that my father had a child with another woman. She had to go and get knocked up with twins—Raymond Jr. and Rayna.

"Dang, Uncle Raymond, I see how you move." Lucci rubbed his hand over the car's shininess. His warm breath against the cold air shot off a vapor fog with each word he spoke.

"As long as you're not afraid of hard work, you can get yourself one of these." Dad tapped the hood with his hand.

"Oh, you bets believe I'll be driving one of these bad boys soon." Lucci's lips formed a devious grin. I could tell he was contemplating something crafty.

"Veronica and I need to get going but be sure to drive safely."

"I will." I waved them off and quickly hopped in the driver's seat. When they drove off, I pulled into their parking space and went back inside the house. I couldn't wait to drive it to school and show it off to my friends.

Mom and I joined the family at the dinner table. Uncle Henry sat at the head of the table and Grandma sat at the opposite end. My great-uncles and great-aunts were still in the living room talking and watching the game. The children sat at their feet, playing with their toys.

"Where is Nolan?" Uncle Henry asked as he scooped up food from each dish that Leslie placed in the center of the table. She sat to my left and Mom sat to my right.

"Oh, he's upstairs, he should have been down here by now," I replied, before putting another forkful of mac 'n' cheese in my mouth. "Leslie, did you make the mac 'n' cheese again this year?"

"I did."

"Girl, you stuck your foot in this once again."

"Thanks."

"I taught my girl well." Grandma winked at Leslie.

"Who made the collard greens?" Mom asked, eating another forkful.

"Naomi, and they're delicious," Grandma said, smiling at

Naomi, who sat to her right and across the table from us. Jasmine was propped on Aunt Naomi's lap so that Boogie could take the empty seat next to her.

"Thank you. I hope the greens aren't too spicy," Aunt Naomi said humbly.

"No, they're delicious. They have just enough kick." Grandma picked up another forkful.

"What about the cabbage I made, Mom? Do you like them?" Mom asked, eyeballing the section of cabbage on Grandma's plate that barely looked touched.

"I tasted them." Grandma said with a bit of a frown. "You're still cooking them in hog meat instead of smoked turkey necks like I told you. I felt my feet swelling up after one bite."

"Still hard to please after all these years," Mom mumbled under her breath.

"Excuse me?" Grandma bucked her eyes. "This is not a competition, Diane."

"I never said it was, Mother."

"You can never let anybody else have the spotlight. Used to do the same thing with your sister. Always competing."

"That's not true," Mom countered.

"It is true. If Irene bought a dress and folks complimented her, you went out and bought a better dress. Irene went to Howard, and you one-upped her and went to Georgetown. You're the reason Irene is mute, and your brother is in jail, so don't get me started."

"Mom, is that true?" I lost my breath for a moment, dropped my fork.

"No, it's not." Mom stood up abruptly, but I wasn't sure what to believe. "I'm not going to sit here and be thrown under a bus. Not today."

She stormed off into the living room.

Leslie and I exchanged looks of concerns. She was probably wondering what I was thinking. *Did my mother do something to Aunt Irene? What was going on with this family? Somebody wasn't telling the truth.*

As we all went back to eating our food, Boogie walked into the dining room.

"Sorry it took me so long."

All heads turned as he sat down wearing Champ's blue and red DeMatha jacket. Uncle Henry's jaw dropped, and his fork clanked against his plate. Something in my gut told me that Uncle Henry's reaction wasn't just about the jacket, but Boogie had made up his face with my makeup. His lashes were thickened with mascara, and he had traced his eyes with eyeliner and his lips with red lipstick. I realized I had left my makeup kit in Aunt Irene's room when my mother called me down to meet my dad.

"Y'all are looking at me like I'm a ghost or something," Boogie sniggered.

"Boogie, you really shouldn't have done that. Not now." Leslie shook her head in dismay.

"I wanted to glam myself like Raven and pay homage to my brother. Don't I look sexy?" Boogie blinked his eyes in dramatic fashion and blew Leslie a kiss.

Uncle Henry sprung up from his chair and slapped Boogie so hard that he fell to the floor. Suddenly, everyone in motion stopped, and then Jasmine erupted into a loud cry. She was just a toddler, but she was smart enough to know that what had happened was wrong. Once she started crying, the other little children started crying too. Leslie quickly took them downstairs to the basement and away from the scene.

"Henry!" Aunt Naomi cried. "Why did you hit your son like that?"

"He's *your* son. My son is dead," Uncle Henry said in a cold tone. He stepped over Boogie like he was dog crap in the street and walked out of the house.

"Oh, heck no! He is not going to do my cousin like that." I jerked up from the table and proceeded to go after Uncle Henry, but my mother came out of the living room and blocked my path to the door.

"Raven, this is Henry's family business, not yours."

"But Mom, Boogie *is* my family. He's my cousin and like a little brother to me."

Mom held up her hand to stop me. "Raven, I get it, but let Henry and Naomi handle this."

I stomped back into the dining room, rolling my eyes, upset.

"...and you shouldn't have been playing like this, Boogie. It's not Halloween, it's Christmas," Grandma was saying to Boogie as she dabbed his bruised cheek with an icepack.

"Who said I was playing?" Boogie grumbled.

"I can't believe your father did this. He has crossed the line and I'm sick of it," Aunt Naomi said, a tear escaping her eye.

"I am too. I hate him!" Boogie stormed off upstairs.

"Boogie, wait." Aunt Naomi ran behind him up the stairs.

My great-uncles went outside to talk to Uncle Henry. I didn't know what else to do. I felt bad for Boogie.

"Let's clean this table off," Mom said to me.

I wanted to ask her more about what Grandma had said earlier regarding her and Aunt Irene, but after what had happened with Boogie, I didn't think I could deal with anything else.

Lucci barged into the house like a hunter trying to catch prey.

"Yo, I heard Unc flicked off on Boogie, is he okay?"

"He's upstairs," I said, wiping the dining room table. Lucci stepped out of the dining room and bumped into Grandma.

"Don't you worry about Boogie. He will be just fine." She patted Lucci on the chest. "Naomi calmed him down, and we don't need you getting him worked up again."

"Alright well, let's everybody move on then. Folks sitting around looking like this is a funeral." Lucci walked over to the stereo and turned on the radio. Donny Hathaway was singing "This Christmas" on 93.9 WKYS.

"Lucci, what's gotten into you? You been smoking them

tweeter things with them no-good boys again?"

He and I both laughed when she said "tweeters."

"What am I going to do with you, boy?"

"Just keep loving me, Grandma. Now come on, let's dance." Lucci took her by the hand and pulled her to the middle of the living room. She looked hesitant at first, but eventually she gave in and the two of them started hand dancing.

"What can I say? The boy is right. We can't let Henry ruin our holiday," Mom said as she walked into the living room. "Who wants to dance with Aunt Di?"

I went to the basement door and called Leslie and the small children back upstairs to join us. I also grabbed Boogie from upstairs. He was hesitant to dance at first but ended up being my dance partner. We all started dancing. The scene was changing in a positive direction. Lucci looked at me and winked. I could only shake my head. He was a trip, but say whatever you want about Lucci, he was funny, and he had a special way of bringing us all back together.

We clapped when the song went off.

"That was fun," Lucci said. I couldn't agree with him more.

We headed outside for our cousin's tradition of making snow angels. Lucci was the first to flop down in all the white fluff. When we finished, we stood up from the ground admiring our artwork.

"One...two...three...four snow angels," Lucci counted with an unsteady finger. "I'm feeling sick."

"That's what you get for drinking and smoking," I laughed sarcastically.

"This is not the final count," Boogie stated, and he lay back down in the snowy yard. He flapped his arms and moved his legs up and down like a windshield wiper. When he finished, there were five snow angels in the snow.

"Now it's complete, with Champ," Boogie whispered.

Leslie and I hugged him and kissed his cheek. We knew

he was still having a challenging time since Champ was gone, but I didn't want the moment to turn somber again, so I put on my best impersonation of Champ and asked...

"My snow angel is the best, right? And what prize do I get?"

Everyone laughed.

"Group hug." Leslie extended her arms. We joined her in a circle and embraced.

"Blood over water, no other relationship before us," Boogie recited our promise.

"I love y'all, but I hate to do this to you." Lucci cringed, and he doubled over, holding his stomach. We jumped out of his way just in time. He upchucked all over our snow angels.

"Man, you ruined it," Boogie sighed.

Lucci hiccupped. "My bad."

"Pew, and you stink." I turned up my nose.

Lucci's head wobbled. "I'm never drinking again."

"Serves you right." Leslie's lips drew in tight and looked like one line. "Come on, let's get you in the house."

Leslie propped his arm over her shoulder, and Boogie and I grabbed his other arm and draped it across us.

"Merry Christmas, guys," Lucci said.

"You too, stinky winky," I laughed.

PART 3

BECOMING YOUNG ADULTS

CHAPTER 17
SPRING FEVER

LESLIE

April 6, 1990

Dear Diary,

Today is Friday. It's the last day of school before Spring Break starts. What felt like the longest winter ever has finally left DC. I sent off my college applications along with my essays. In case Grandma doesn't want me to go away to school, I decided at the last minute to apply to Howard University. She may like that since Mama went to school there.

Grandma said Mama wanted to be a schoolteacher, but she had me during her senior year and never got to finish. I hope to do everything that Mama didn't get a chance to do, except I want to become a writer instead of a schoolteacher.

I asked Aunt Diane what happened between her and Mama and all she said was, "The past should stay in the past." I don't know why it's such a big secret. I guess I will never learn the whole truth about Mama.

Lucci got his Acura fixed. He added brand new rims, and a stereo. He doesn't have a job, so I know the money wasn't made legally. His father gave him a tongue lashing on the phone after Grandma told him he hangs out with thugs. All they do is smoke, drink, fight, and get into trouble. His dad told him to find new friends and to get his life together. Beanz, who lives down the street is a cool buddy of his. But even Beanz said he didn't think Mook and Peanut were good friends for Lucci. Speaking of Lucci, he just tooted the horn. We need to get to school. I'll keep Lucci in my prayers. Only God can save him.

—Leslie

"You were about to get left." Lucci's eyes stared at me intensely.

"You wouldn't have left me."

"Try that crap next time, and you gonna mess around and find out," he snapped, pulling his black LA Raiders cap over his freshly cornrowed hair. His girlfriend Keisha came over yesterday and braided it for him. He'd gotten rid of the box Philly haircut in the 80s.

N.W.A was playing from the tape deck. I recognized their voices because I'd heard someone playing their music at school. The rappers spewed profanity and talked about women using derogatory names.

"Can we listen to something that doesn't have misogynist lyrics?"

"Nah, we ain't listening to nothing else," Lucci retorted. "When you get your own whip, you can play whatever you want." He leaned so far back in the driver's seat that people probably thought the car was driving by itself and I was just a passenger.

"I don't need a car when I'm about to go away to college."

"Girl, you ain't going nowhere."

"I'm going far away from here."

He laughed cynically. "Grandma barely let you off the front porch!"

"She'll make an exception for college I hope, but Howard will be my last option if she doesn't."

"You let her treat you like Cinderella."

"Maybe if you help us out, I wouldn't have to be." I rolled my eyes.

"I do my part, but I ain't letting nobody use me."

"You take out the trash and that's it. You should do more. She lets you live with her scot-free."

"I'm her grandson, not a maid, and I don't owe her for that and neither do you."

"What is that supposed to mean?"

He leaned forward and turned the music down. "It's not your fault what happened to your mother, but Grandma is making you responsible for her."

"She *is* my mother, and Grandma needs my help."

"If you do all the cooking, cleaning, laundry, and errands, what does Grandma do? Sounds like more than help to me."

"The bigger question is, what is it that *you* do?"

"Don't try to twist this on me. I'm talking about you, Cuz," Lucci raised his voice to emphasize his point. "You're eighteen, but you don't even have a driver's license. You've never been on a date, and you don't go out with friends. Are you even allowed to go to your senior prom this year?"

"Please don't patronize me, it's impolite."

"Can you stop using those big words?"

"What big words?"

"*Patronize* and *misogyny*. No need to get all *Jeopardy* on me. Anyway," he blew hot air through his lip. "You need to open your eyes. Grandma is not a saint. She may complain about me to my father, but she takes the money I give her. And she also gets a check for you and *your* mother. Yet, Aunt Diane buys all your clothes. Where does the rest of the money go?"

"I don't want to continue this conversation. I love Grandma. I'm not going to talk about her behind her back like this. She takes care of both of us and uses the money for food and to pay bills. You need to be appreciative and show her some respect."

"Cuz, sometimes our enemies are the ones in our own household. You're blind to how Grandma uses you. That's why you don't have a life."

"I'm not blind to anything, but you have been ungrateful."

He parked the car in Eastern's parking lot, and when I got out, I slammed the door behind me and hurried into the school building. The conversation made me deeply upset.

As soon as I closed my locker door, I caught the big, handsome eyes of Michael West looking at me. He was standing in front of his locker about ten footsteps away from mine. A smile came over his face and he winked at me. I returned an unwavering smile that didn't quite reach my eyes. *What was that all about?*

"Hey Leslie, wait up!" The bass of Michael's voice echoed down the hall, as I headed to first period. I paused, turned around, and gave him a look that said *What do you want?*

"You're headed to Ms. Mackle's class, right?" He raised a bushy eyebrow. I nodded yes. "I'll walk you."

A few onlookers who were lingering in the hallway gawked at us walking together. They were probably wondering what I was thinking. *Why is Michael showing interest in me?*

"You look nice today," Michael flirted. I was only wearing a casual Cross Colours jumper with a T-shirt that Aunt Diane had bought me for my birthday.

"Thanks." I sped up my walk to the point I was almost skipping.

"I was wondering if you wouldn't mind helping me write my paper for senior midterms?"

This is why he's suddenly interested in me?

"Look, if you needed help with your paper, all you had to do was ask."

Michael threw up his hands. "Chill, my bad."

"I offer tutoring in Mr. Hill's classroom on Fridays during lunch."

"Thanks, Big Leslie, you're the best." He whacked my shoulder like I was his football teammate and rushed off. I hurried to Ms. Mackle's chemistry class just as the nine o'clock bell rang.

I joined KC and two other classmates at one of the lab tables, plopping my textbook down so hard that the test tubes rattled.

"Glad you could make it in the nick of time, Ms. Walker," Ms. Mackle stated, staring at me over her dark-framed glasses. I rolled my eyes. I hated that she put me on the spot.

KC leaned in and whispered, "Are you OK?"

My jaw tightened. "Everything is fine and dandy."

KC glared at me with concern. She knew I wasn't fine, but life was good for her and everybody else, never for me. I still felt unsettled about the car conversation with Lucci. I couldn't concentrate as Ms. Mackle finished writing out formulas and decided to give us a pop quiz. *Really?* I huffed under my breath as I pulled out a pencil from my backpack.

Lucci's question about the prom came to my mind. I didn't have a date. I wondered if it was because I was fat that no one asked me. Michael's comment floated through my mind. *Thanks, BIG Leslie.* If I was skinny like KC or Raven, would people treat me with more respect? No one ever says, hey *skinny* girl, it's always *big* girl. Why is that?

At lunchtime, I wanted to eat alone, but when I looked up, KC was headed my way. She was dressed to the nines, hair and nails done. I watched as all the guys' eyes follow her like a mouse chasing cheese in a maze, as she walked across the cafeteria. They never looked at me like that. I wasn't even an afterthought.

"Hey, mind if I join you?" KC asked perkily.

"It's a free country."

She narrowed her eyes suspiciously. "Are you sure you're okay?"

I stuffed my mouth with a few overcooked french fries and swallowed its bitterness.

"I'm fine."

"Okay, well, I've been meaning to tell you about a guy I've been seeing lately. His name is Devante, and he goes to H.D. Woodson."

"How did you meet him?" I asked nonchalantly.

"We were volunteering together at a homeless shelter last month. We've been dating ever since. He just asked me to be his girlfriend."

"Good for you." I slurped my soda, making a loud suction noise on purpose.

"We're going to the prom together next month," she squealed. "I can't wait!"

"I'm happy for you." I forced a smile like a corny game-show host.

"Say, you should come with us next week. We're going to see the movie *House Party* with Kid 'n Play."

I jerked my head back. "And be a third wheel?"

KC huffed impatiently. "Of course not. I was just hoping you would join us to have some fun."

"You just want to show off your new boyfriend."

"What's wrong with you, Leslie? You know what. Just forget I even asked."

Brriiiiing.

The loud bell sounded to end lunch and start fifth period.

By the time I tossed my empty food wrappings in the trash, KC was halfway down the hall. I felt kind of bad for the way I had been acting toward her. Lucci was right. I didn't have a life. Perhaps it was time to change that.

"Hey KC, wait up!"

CHAPTER 18
ROBBING

LUCCI

April 11, 1990

As-Salamu-'Alaikum Donovan!

I'm writing because I am still concerned as to why you have not written back to me nor been around to accept my collect calls. Son, I hate to sound like I'm always lecturing you, but I only want what is best for you. There is no future in being a thug except jail or the grave.

Look at me, I am living as an example of that. I have served nearly 16 years for a crime I never committed. Because of my reputation it was easy for the judge to throw me in prison. On the streets they called me "Hammer" because I did hits for drug dealers, pimps, and gamblers, including Turk and Theresa. I did get involved in the drug game too, but I never killed anyone.

I'm a changed man now. I'm no longer angry. I don't drink or smoke, and I'm not violent anymore, thank God. Your Aunt Diane got her friend Gerald to help appeal my case because she knows I am an innocent man. No one ever found the weapon that supposedly killed the person they said I killed, but I do know who did it. I'm omitting the name and details for the sake of my appeal. However, not a day goes by when I don't think about being FREE. I want the chance to be a father to you. If it's too late when I get out, I would at least want to be your friend.

Please son, take advantage of your life and all the

opportunities that you have. Don't be like me. I had both parents in my life and a roof over my head, but I still chose the streets. You don't have to. Your grandmother loves you, your aunts, and your uncle love you, and especially your cousins. What about them? I thought you told me you were going to try to be a good example to them after Champ died. What happened to that promise?

All the money and riches in the world will never be able to get you your freedom back when it's gone. I had money, cars, women, jewelry, and respect in the streets, but none of that crap could stop me from going to prison. It's time for you to get your life together, Donovan. Be grateful for what you have before you wish you had. We all reap what we sow. I hope I sowed seeds of knowledge in you to do better because you deserve better. You ARE better than what you're doing. You have the freedom I wish I had never lost because it meant losing you. I'm begging you, son, please change your life. You don't want to end up where I am. Prison is a horrible place.

I wish you well my son and give my love to the family.

As-Salamu-'Alaikum
Donovan X

I balled up the letter from my father and tossed it in the trash can. Mook and Peanut were waiting for me outside. Grandma didn't allow them in the house anymore. She said they smoked and drank too much. Mook and Peanut were my homies. She viewed them as thugs, but I considered them my friends.

I grabbed my gun from the shoebox and tucked it in the front of my pants. It was time to go score some more money. Thus far, we've been robbing nearly every drug dealer hustling on the strips. I didn't need to hustle for Turk or anyone else, my job was easy. Aim, threaten, and take the money. Tonight was going to be our biggest score, and I was going to use the money to buy a new whip like

Raven, and to make a rap album at a studio out in B-More. Folks are going to call me the next Ice Cube. I ran upstairs from the basement toward the front door.

"See ya later, Grams!" I threw up the peace sign with my fingers and rushed out of the door.

"Did you even read your father's letter that I gave you?" Grandma came to the door, yelling behind me.

I looked over my shoulder, nodded. "Yeah, I read it."

"Well, when you come back, the doors will be locked."

"You're kicking me out?" I asked. She had already taken my house keys from me last week.

"I don't have a choice, do I?" She propped her hand on her hip.

"I promise I'll be back before my midnight curfew this time, and I'll give you some more money for your troubles."

"Money for *my* troubles? Lucci, I've been saving that money you gave me in case I need it one day to bail you out of jail. If you don't end up there, I'll give it back to you." She went back inside and slammed the door. I felt terrible. All this time I assumed she had been using my money for herself.

BEEP' BEEP'

"Come on!" Mook yelled. I hopped in on the passenger's side of the hoopty that Mook, Peanut, and I had stolen. I never rode in my own whip whenever I was pulling a lick.

"Yo, your grandmother be tripping and bugging out just like mine," Mook said.

"Mine too. After a while, she sounds like one of them Charlie Brown conversations from the Peanuts. '*Whomp, whomp, whomp,*'" Peanut emitted from the back seat, and the three of us cracked up laughing. Deep inside I was feeling uneasy after that exchange with my grandmother, but I had no time to dwell on it.

Tonight, we were going to rob the Northeast hustlers in Ivy City who hung out on Montana Avenue. We'd been clocking them and learning their schedules. A buddy of mine named Dre, who used to hustle for Turk down Capers told us some New York dudes were making a drop tonight. We didn't want the drugs and never took them, at least I never did. I always went after the cash.

Anyway, Dre told me there would be an exchange at midnight in Montana Terrace projects. I promised Dre we'd give him a percentage for setting up the score. Dre had been a corner boy like us, but he moved his way up the ranks. He said he was a hitter for one of the dealers and would be standing guard during the transaction. That way, it wouldn't look like he had anything to do with the robbery. I figured our plan was perfect.

We drove over to Northeast and circled the block until we got the page from Dre that the New York dudes were on their way. About an hour later, my pager went off with the code 4-4-8, which spelled out HIT on a phone keypad.

"This is it, fellas. Time to make our move and do it fast," I said eagerly, and Mook parked the black paper-tagged hoopty on 15th Street NE near an alley. That way, we could easily get away fast.

We hopped out of the car and ran up the hill toward the Montana Terrace apartment housing projects on the left. Once we got to the top, we slowed down and played it off like we were casually walking the block, as if we lived near there. We turned down the open pathway that led to a courtyard. A group of dudes ahead of us were hustling near the dumpsters, so we quickly turned the corner and went the other way, around the backend of the building.

Once inside building 888-B, we donned our ski masks and withdrew our Ninas. It was quiet inside the building, but then suddenly, someone inside their apartment started playing "Tomorrow" by Tevin Campbell. As we climbed the steps, the music got louder, as if they were turning it up on purpose. The song made me think about my father's letter when he said, *you are better than what you're doing.*

"Man, I wish they'd turn that crap off," I said, just loud enough for Mook and Peanut to hear me as we crept up the stairs.

"Nah, it's perfect. They won't hear us," Mook responded.

When we got to apartment 4A, Peanut and I gave Mook the head nod that it was the right unit. Mook, who was well over three-hundred pounds, kicked in the apartment door. It crashed to the floor. He rushed inside with his gun aimed straight ahead. Peanut and I rushed in behind him with our guns drawn. There were two Latino-looking dealers who were counting money on the living room table while one guy stood on guard by the sofa. Mook shouted for them to put their hands in the air while Peanut rushed over to pat them down and took their weapons. I stood guard at the entryway where the front door used to be while Peanut and Mook tied up the guys with rope and duct tape. I dared them not to move or even flinch. I counted three people in the room. There were two dealers and only one guard. My stomach felt queasy. *Where is Dre? There is supposed to be two guards not just one. This count doesn't make sense.*

"Man, look at all this money!" Mook kissed the stacks as he and Peanut quickly loaded the duffle bag that was already on the table. While they were stacking the money in the bag, I saw a shadow of a person move from my peripheral vision to my right.

"Let's go! Somebody else is in here," I shouted.

"Where?" Mook and Peanut looked over their shoulders.

"Right here!"

POW, POW.

It was Dre, and he fired off shots that knocked Mook and Peanut to the floor. My jaw dropped in shock! Their heads cocked to the side, and I knew they were gone. Dre turned toward me, aiming his gun. My eyes stretched opened wider, and my lips trembled as life and death flashed before my eyes. I knew it was going to be Dre or me. I quickly chose me...

CHAPTER 19
LOTUS FLOWER

RAVEN

A palette of blue and purple
feathering a blue sky
gentle as teardrops
falling from my eyes
a replica of half moons
dazzling a yellow bloom
the sun sets to bring the night
as shooting stars zoom
I wonder where you are
I listen to Earth sleep
night crawlers creeping
wrestling the fall leaves
it's not your season yet
those who want you will wait
you're a lady in radiant purple
your victory doesn't come late
you lie amongst the green
gracing the lake scene
beauty in three-dimensional circles
along the water stream
we must be ready for your hour
when you come in the full bloom
oh beautiful lotus flower.

"What do you think?" I asked Adrian.

He sat next to me on my sofa. We'd been hanging out all spring break.

"It's as beautiful as you." Adrian smiled.

"Aw, you're just saying that because you like me."

"True, but I really think you've got a knack for poetry."

"Thank you." I blushed as I closed my composition book. I'd been practicing writing poems since Mom had been so preoccupied with Gerald.

"Do you have a date for your senior prom?" I asked.

"Not yet, but—"

"Good. Leslie needs a prom date."

Adrian heaved a long sigh. "Raven, why do you keep trying to hook me up with your cousin?"

"Because she needs a prom date."

He glared at me through his thin-framed glasses. "I don't want to go out with Leslie or any other girl except you."

"But we're good friends."

He scooted closer to me, closing the gap between us. "I was hoping that you wouldn't mind being my prom date."

"Are we going just as friends?"

He twisted his lips and groaned. "I guess so."

"Good. If you understand we're friends, I'll go with you. Now we need to go shopping so I can pick out a dress and you can buy a tux. Our colors will be fuchsia and black."

"What about blue and black?"

"Nope. Fuchsia and black."

"Fine. Fuchsia and black it is!"

"I'll call my cousin Boogie. He has good fashion taste too. He can join us and help find the colors we need."

"But I was hoping that it would be just you and me," he kissed the back of my hand.

"Boogie is coming with us."

"Okay, fine. Boogie can come. Let's go pick him up." Adrian threw up his hands, giving into my every whim.

"Awesome! We can use my dad's credit card to pay for everything."

"Are you sure he'd be cool about that? I heard prom attire can be expensive."

"He doesn't have a choice. He missed his visitation week with me last weekend because he's been working on another corporate case. It's how he always makes it up to

133

me. He leaves me with his credit card, but sets a budget limit," I explained.

"Wow, I wish my dad had that much trust in me," he said. "You know, having you as my date will make me the coolest dude at St. Francis."

"And I hope by being your date it will make us King and Queen of your prom."

CHAPTER 20
SPRING SHOPPING

BOOGIE

My father had started having heated arguments with my mother to the point I'd call the police out of fear that he was going to hurt her or me. It was high time Mom left him. Mom didn't want anything from my father except full custody of my sister Jasmine and me, but her lawyer, who was a bulldog like Aunt Diane, told her to seek child support and alimony. Mom followed her lawyer's advice and won the case. Dad got to keep the house in Maryland and Mom got us kids. We moved to DC and rented a house on Kentucky Avenue with the option to buy. Unbeknownst to me, Mom had filed for divorce after Christmas and started house hunting shortly afterward. I overheard her sharing the details with one of her girlfriends on the phone, but to our family, it seemed like it all happened too fast. Mom had always wanted to be closer to her teaching job at Hine Junior High School in DC, so it worked out.

Thanks to Aunt Diane, the civil case for victim's restitution against Theophilus Duckworth and the Maynard Billard Construction Company never went to trial. They decided to settle out of court. I never knew how much the settlement was for, but mom said Jasmine and I wouldn't have to pay for college. She's been furnishing the house and bought a brand-new Nissan Maximum.

Living around the corner from Grandma's house is nice. We get to see the family more often. In the mornings, we drop Jasmine off at Little People's Paradise Daycare on 15th Street. Jasmine is four now, and I'm 15 in ninth grade. I started Hine right after spring break. Most of the students knew my mom for teaching seventh-grade English. I knew I still had to stay on my best behavior and do well in my classes since Mom taught there. So far, life is getting better for us. I still miss Champ every day, but at least things are peaceful with my father gone.

"How do I look?" Raven asked, standing before the mirror on my dresser. She'd come over to pick me up to shop for the prom.

"Work it, girl. You are always gorgeous. Why are you checking the mirror?"

"I need to make sure I look fly for a cute guy at the mall."

"But what about Adrian?" I whispered, knowing he was downstairs waiting for us.

"What about him?"

"Girl, you know he likes you. Stop being a tease before you lose him."

"I got him wrapped around my fingers."

"Don't say I didn't warn you."

"I've been warned, and I don't care."

"Did you remember to bring your dad's credit card?"

"Right here." She withdrew it from her purse.

"Retail therapy here we come!"

At Pentagon City mall, we found Raven a dress and Adrian a tuxedo, and afterward, we shopped for ourselves. We went to every single store. Honey, we were charging up everything! Adrian eventually did a beeline to the bench in the concourse. He was exhausted from shopping with us.

"Wait, before we go, we have to hit up Sam Goody and get some music." I grabbed Raven's hand.

"But we charged over five hundred dollars already," Raven's eyes jumped with worry.

"Already? Dang! Well, let's go then. I don't want you to get in trouble."

"Perhaps a hundred more dollars wouldn't hurt,"

Raven's forehead wrinkled with doubt as she bit down on her bottom lip.

"Cool. Let's go!"

I went straight toward the House/Party Music aisle while Raven went to the R&B section. I grabbed C+C Music Factory and SNAP.

"Hi, aren't you Nolan from Hine?" asked a short, light-skinned girl about my height with long hair and pretty eyes.

"Nicole, right?" I asked to be sure. I was new to Hine, but I recalled seeing her in geography class. She always wore Daisy Duke shorts that I liked.

"I thought that was you. You're the only guy at school who dresses so fly and have a nice curly fade." She beamed.

"That's me," I clucked my tongue.

"I saw your name on the list of performers for the upcoming talent show. Are you dancing to C+C Music Factory?" she asked, gazing at their album in my hand.

"You know it. Are you performing too?"

"I can't dance with these two left feet," she gushed.

Raven walked over and stood next to me.

"Oh, this is my—"

"Girlfriend?" Nicole asked, sounding a bit disappointed.

"No, she's my cousin Raven. Raven, this is Nicole."

"It's nice to meet you!" Raven spoke, acting overly bubbly.

"You too," Nicole's face relaxed. "Nolan, let me give you my number. I'd like you to teach me how to dance."

"I'd love too." My eyes danced with hers, as she took my hand and wrote her number on my palm.

"You can call me Boogie, everyone else does."

"Bye Boogie." she leaned in and tenderly kissed my cheek. Walked away with her friends.

Raven's mouth dropped. "Uhm, what was that about?"

I shrugged. "Nothing. We go to Hine together."

"You know she likes you."

"She's just being friendly that's all."

"Not with a kiss like that!" Raven instigated. "So, what are you going to tell her?"

"About what?"

"Come on, Cuz. You *know* you *don't* get down like that."

I flipped up my hand, rolled my neck. "Hold up, you think you know me?"

"Yes! I've known you all of your life."

Raven followed me to the counter and paid for our music, but she wouldn't let up on the topic.

"Are you going to tell her?" she pressed.

"There's nothing to tell when I don't even know myself."

"Seriously?"

"Look girl, stay in your lane. This is my business."

"So, it's like that? I thought...I thought we were best friends."

"We are, but like my mom always says, even friends have to draw a line in the sand sometimes."

"Fine." Raven pouted her lips. But honey, she would have to get over it.

CHAPTER 21
GO WHERE THERE IS LOVE

LUCCI

The night I fled Montana Avenue, I let the hoopty coast into the Potomac River. Tossed my gun right behind it. Been couch-surfing and running out of money ever since. Should've taken the money at the last lick, but I got scared after shooting Dre. Don't even know if he's dead or alive. He could be looking for me. Didn't want to contact Turk but I was in trouble, so I paged him from a pay phone outside of a Sunoco gas station at the bottom of the Sousa Bridge.

While I waited for Turk to call me back, I went inside to grab something to drink and a snack. A TV behind the fiberglass counter where the cashier sat was playing loud. I overheard the news reporter.

"The police may have more information about what happened last week in Montana Terrace Apartments in Northeast. Police said the scene looked like an armed robbery attempt in a drug deal that went bad. In this double homicide case, the police said they found ski masks on the two deceased who have been identified as minors. Their next of kin have been notified. Another young Black man was found shot in the neck inside this same apartment. He remains in the hospital in critical condition. Because this is an ongoing investigation involving minors, we are unable to release names. However, several witnesses say they saw a black car with tinted windows and paper tags JY9809 speeding away from the scene. Police are urging those who know anything about this case to call the Crime Solvers hotline."

The payphone rang outside. I tossed my last five dollars through the plexiglass to pay for my BonTon chips and hot sausage. I rushed outside to answer it.

"Hello?"

"Yo, who dis?" the voice on the other end asked. I figured he was one of Turk's lieutenants.

"It's Lucci. I'm in trouble and I need Turk ASAP."

I could hear him covering the phone with his hand and mumbling something in the background before Turk picked up.

"Talk," Turk commanded.

"I messed up, Cuz, and I need help."

"Are you serious right now?"

"Yeah, I know. I'm a knucklehead and I haven't been keeping my head on a swivel and blah blah blah...I need help, man."

"A little birdie told me you're a stickup kid."

"I don't do that no more," I said, looking over my shoulder making sure I didn't see any cops driving by.

"You been robbing dudes in Potomac Gardens, Kentucky Court, and Capers."

"What are you talking about?"

"Don't play dumb with me!" he shouted. "When you robbed my young soldiers, you were taking money from me."

I briefly took the phone from my ear and tried to figure out how he knew. As if he was reading my mind, he said, "I told you to watch the company you keep. Peanut from your crew is a rat. He told Marcia how you guys have been getting money, and Angel told a lieutenant of mine."

Peanut? He was messing with Marcia behind my back? How could he do me like that? I thought we was homies. Guess it don't matter now.

"You're a dead man walking, Lucci. If you weren't family, I'd kill you myself!"

I wiped the nervous sweat from my forehead and switched the phone to my other ear. Now I was scared more than ever. My heart was beating so hard I could feel it pounding in my throat.

"You're involved in that hit over on Montana Avenue, aren't you? That's why you're calling me."

I swallowed hard and tried to stop shaking as I held the phone. "Dre killed Peanut and Mook, then turned his gun on me. I ain't have a choice."

"There's always a choice. Yours should've been not to engage in the situation in the first place," he spat. "You crossed the line this time. Those Northeast cats are connected to New York dealers. That means they're probably already down here looking for you. I don't need that heat coming my way. Matter of fact, I'm hanging up so I can go buy Theresa that black dress."

Click.

Turk hung up the phone. I tried to collect myself as I walked across the street to take the bus home. Never been so scared in my whole life. Should've listened to my father. Should've listened to my grandmother too.

Leslie opened the front door wearing a robe with pajamas underneath. She looked surprised to see me, but I never felt so glad to see her. Just being home, a warm feeling of safety came over me. It was then that I remembered Turk's word from when I was a kid. *Go where there is love.* My grandmother's house was a place of peace and love. Despite all our family drama, there was love in the midst. I knew that now more than ever before.

"Lucci, we've been looking all over for you!" Leslie pulled me inside and shut the door. I asked where Grandma was and she said bingo.

"You don't look right. What's going on?" Leslie's eyes traced over me with concern.

I got choked up at the thought of never seeing her again. My eyes watered and my hands shook at my sides. I had targets on my back. The way I saw it, I was going to be dead by either Turk's soldiers, Mook and Peanuts' family who thought I killed them, or the New York dealers coming for me. I couldn't stay with Grandma and Leslie anymore. They didn't deserve to get caught up in my mess.

"What did you do, Lucci?" Leslie's voice cracked. I found it hard to say the words to what I'd done. My lips trembled as I told her everything that happened in case I got smoked. She would be the one who knew the truth.

"...and I'm sorry for all the trouble I caused you and Grandma," I sniffed, swallowing my salty tears.

Leslie tenderly grabbed my hands and started praying for me. I felt it this time. In my mind and heart, I asked God to forgive me...

CHAPTER 22
WHEN IT'S TIME

LESLIE

April 23, 1990

Dear Diary,

We don't know where Lucci is. When he came home the other night and told me what happened, I woke up the next morning and he was gone. I had no choice but to tell my family what I knew.

Unfortunately, my spring break was spent looking for Lucci with Uncle Henry, who is back on the force. Aunt Diane and my cousins came with us, too. We never found him. I pray to God that he is somewhere safe.

Lucci's friends Mook and Peanut are dead. Uncle Henry said the streets were talking, and folks said Lucci shot Mook and Peanut, but I knew Lucci wouldn't do that. Those guys were his friends. He did tell me that he shot Dre in self-defense. According to the news and Uncle Henry, Dre is in critical condition. Uncle Henry said if Dre dies, Lucci will go to jail for murder! Uncle Donovan has been calling collect every day asking if Lucci has turned up yet. We're all scared for Lucci. He's in big trouble this time!

-Leslie

The loud sound of a lawn mower rumbled outside my bedroom window, interrupting my journaling thoughts. I closed my diary and stepped out of bed to look out the window. I spotted a shirtless Mitch mowing our grass in the backyard. He was wearing a bucket-style Madness hat. His stomach glistened with sweat, looking like a layered plane of muscles, and his biceps appeared sculpted as if he'd been lifting heavy objects in reps of a hundred.

"Lord, please forgive me for lusting," I prayed under my breath, but my eyes were locked on his body. Normally, grass cutting was Lucci's responsibility, but Lucci wasn't here. I figured Grandma must've asked Mitch to do it instead.

Mitch must have sensed someone looking at him because he looked up at the window. I waved. He responded with a quick wave and continued mowing the lawn. Mitch hadn't been the same since he found out Angel cheated on him, and there was no baby. I had overheard him sharing the news with Lucci a while back. Angel was a fool to cheat on Mitch. He was such a nice guy. When I was walking home with KC the other day, she pointed Angel out to me. Angel was kissing a well-known drug dealer on 15th Street by the carryout. KC said he had bought Angel a BMW. It seems to me that Angel is a gold digger. Mitch didn't need her using him anymore.

I closed the curtains and slipped on a T-shirt and a jean skirt and stepped my feet into a pair of slides. I figured Mitch had to be thirsty from all his hard work, so I went downstairs to the kitchen and poured him a glass of cold lemonade.

It felt hotter than usual for a spring day. Grass was flying everywhere, making my throat itch and nose twitch. As I approached Mitch, he turned the motor off.

"Hey, I brought you some lemonade."

"Thanks." He quickly gulped it down in just a few swallows.

"I never got a chance to say it, but I'm sorry about you and Angel's breakup," I said as gently as I could. "I left you a couple of messages on your answering machine."

Mitch removed his garden gloves and wiped the sweat

off his forehead. "Are you really sorry or just being polite?"

I was taken aback. "What do you mean?"

"A few months ago, it seemed like you weren't too happy when I told you Angel was pregnant."

My hands clammed up, and my heart raced with alarm. I felt attacked.

"And I got your messages. I wasn't ready to talk to anybody, and if it's okay with you, I don't want to talk about Angel ever again."

"Leslie!" Grandma called, interrupting. She stood at the back door, yelling through the screen. "You've got mail from these darn colleges again. I don't know why they keep writing to you. You're not going out of state."

I walked over to retrieve my mail.

"Mitch are you almost done?" she asked. "I'm about to go play my numbers at Al's Liquor Store."

"Almost done," Mitch replied, glancing over a half-cut yard.

Grandma reached inside her bra for her small change purse to pay Mitch. He walked over, and she handed him a ten-dollar bill and went back inside.

I flipped through the letters in my hand. This time, they were letters from the schools I'd applied to and not just colleges soliciting me.

"You got offers from college, huh?" Mitch stepped in closer to snoop.

"No sense in me opening them," I lamented.

"Why not?"

"It's too much going on here. I'm sure you've heard about Lucci's situation since Grandma talks to your mom."

"I have, but how is he your problem?"

I was losing my patience with Mitch. "Because he's my cousin, that's why!"

"Sheesh, don't bite my head off." He threw up his hands.

"I should be telling *you* that."

"Listen, I'm sorry. I didn't mean to snap at you a moment ago. I just wanted you to be honest with me."

"Honest about what?"

"Forget it," he shook his head.

"Okay. Well, how come you never went to college?"

"School was never my thing." He shrugged.

"Don't you need a degree to become a store manager?"

"No, only a GED or a high school diploma," he said, then puckered his brow. "Say, you remembered I wanted to be a store manager?"

"Uh-hah. I remember everything about you."

"Why? I'm nobody special."

"You are special. God made us all that way."

"Anyway, there's been a change in my plans now."

"Really?"

"I'm joining the Navy. I'll be flying out to San Diego late July for bootcamp."

I blinked in shock as if someone had just slapped me. "

"I got no reason to stay here anymore." His tone sounded like he was still wounded from Angel.

"Is your mom okay with you going away to the Navy?"

"She encouraged it."

I swallowed down the disappointment. I had found comfort in knowing that Mitch would always be right across the street, and now he was leaving me.

"Your grandmother may have told you this, but in case she didn't, my mom got engaged to Bernard last week."

"Yes, I heard. How do you feel about that?"

"He's a good dude. You will see a For Sale sign in our front yard this summer," he smiled. "They're buying a house in Virginia closer to my mom's new job at Elder Care Hospital."

My head was spinning. This was all happening too soon. I couldn't believe Mitch was leaving me, and his mother was moving away. They had been our neighbors since I was a kid. I still remember when Mitch first moved in. Champ was the first to invite Mitch over to play with us. He'd been like family ever since.

"Well, I'd better finish up this yard."

I quickly leaned in and kissed his cheek.

Mitch lifted his eyebrows in surprise, and with a half grin he asked, "What was that about?"

"I'm sorry." I covered my mouth with my hand.

"No, you're not. See, that's what I meant by being honest. You should never feel sorry about how you truly feel." He leaned down and planted a tender kiss on my lips and held it a few seconds. "Hopefully, that's better than last time."

"You remember our kiss?" I blushed.

"I remember everything about you as much as you remember everything about me."

I crossed my arms, twisted my lips. "Sure, you do. Are you pulling my leg?"

"Oh, come on, girl, don't play me like that when I've known you all of your life."

"I'm listening."

"Okay fine. I know you cook for your family, study with KC, and you read novels. Oh, according to Raven, you keep a diary of all the crazy crap that happens in your family."

"Well, I hope this means you won't forget about me when you're in the Navy."

"I don't plan to." His eyes swayed with mine, then he leaned down to pick up his garden gloves. I stepped closer to kiss him again, but I didn't want to seem too fresh. I stopped myself a few inches away. Played it off by pulling a string of my hair behind my ear instead.

"Besides, I think it'll be kind of cool if we create some new memories together before I go."

"What did you have in mind?" I batted my eyes.

"Bike riding. I fixed that old bus you got in the shed," he revealed. "When I was grabbing the lawn mower, I figured you must've stopped riding it when the chain popped, so I fixed it."

I turned up my nose. "What kind of date is that?"

"Don't worry. It'll be fun." He winked.

"If you say so."

CHAPTER 23
GROWING PAINS

RAVEN

I felt so angry that I could spit fire like a dragon. My hair was flying with the wind as the wheels of my convertible Mercedes sped down the 495 highway. Wilson Philipps crooned "Hold On" from my car stereo. I eased up on the gas when I noticed traffic ahead of me. I decided to give Adrian a call to vent.

"Hello?" he answered.

"Adrian, you're not going to believe this!"

"Hey Rave, I'm on another call."

"We need to talk like right now," I insisted.

"But I have someone on hold."

"*This* is urgent."

He heaved a sigh. "Fine, hold on."

The phone silenced a moment and then he came back.

"What's going on?"

"Gerald and Mom took me to breakfast this morning at the Red Barn."

"Is that it?"

"No. They asked for my blessing in marriage. This is so unfair. Mom and I were just having so much fun together. Now I have to share her with him?"

"Raven, don't you think you're being a little bit selfish."

"Are you taking their side?"

"This isn't about taking sides. I think if they're in love they deserve to be happy."

I gritted my teeth. "I expected you to understand. I guess I'll explain it to my father when I get to his house."

"Sorry you didn't get the answer you hoped for, but—"

"Who were you talking to on the other line?" I asked, bluntly, as I got off at the next exit.

"Uh...about that..."

"Spit it out!"

"Hold on, sheesh!" he sounded frustrated. "I'm seeing Zoey, alright?"

"Zoey? Zoey who is on the cheerleading squad with me?"

"Yes."

"I guess going with you to your prom made you popular after all huh?"

"Guess so," he replied, and I could almost see a big goofy braces smile on his face.

"You're a trader!"

"What?" he gasped. "How am I a trader? You said you wanted to be friends."

"We are but—" *I wasn't expecting you to end up with someone else.*

"But what?"

"Nothing. If you want to be with Zoey, you go right ahead and see if I care."

"Raven, Taj wasn't right for cheating on you, but he was right when he said you're a spoiled brat."

"Excuse me?"

"You heard me. You're spoiled and you're selfish, and it's better for us not to be friends anymore. Mitch was right too. He said I needed to stand up to you, so there, I said it!"

"Mitch? You've been talking to Mitch?"

"Yes, we play ball together sometimes."

"He needs to mind his own business."

"He was. I asked *him* for advice about you."

"Fine. You and Mitch can shove your advice where the sun doesn't shine!"

"You're so immature, Rave."

"What-*ever.*"

Click.

I hung up on Adrian. Some friend he was!

* * *

I arrived at Dad's colonial style house in Silver Spring and parked in his driveway in front of his double-car garage. I used the spare key he gave me, and I marched right inside.

"Why, hello Raven." Veronica's arched eyebrow was raised in surprise to see me. She wore an apron and appeared to be cooking dinner from the open kitchen while the twins were inside their playpen in the living room, but within her eye view.

"Where's my father?"

"Hello to you, too," Veronica set her kitchen mitten aside and hurried over to me. "Is everything alright?"

"It's none of your business."

Veronica tilted her head and clutched her chest. "Excuse me? Don't you dare speak to me in that tone."

"Raven, is that you? I'm back here," Dad shouted from his office down the hall. It was a den, but he'd turned it into his office.

"Move out of my way," I brushed past Veronica and nearly took her shoulder with me.

"Raven, I really don't appreciate you barging in on us like this," Veronica bellowed out.

"Talk to the hand." I flipped my palm in her face just as I walked into Dad's office.

"Girl I will—"

"Stop, Veronica. I got it from here." Dad abruptly stood up from his desk.

"Raymond, I will *not* tolerate this type of disrespect!"

"I will handle it from here, sweetheart. Go ahead and finish dinner. I got it."

Veronica stormed out of the office fuming obscenities under her breath as Dad sat back down behind his desk. I took the seat in front of it.

"Raven, what's gotten into you? If this is about you and Taj's breakup, you need to get over it. You had no right to come in here with that disrespect."

"Dad, I've been over Taj. He's old news, but Adrian is seeing my friend Zoey on the cheerleading squad. And just this morning, Mom and Gerald asked for my blessing in marriage. This is all too much. My life is going crazy dad!"

He removed his glasses and wiped the sweat from his forehead. His desk was a cluttery mess. He was working on another big corporate case and looked stressed out.

"Life happens, Raven. You have to learn to accept its changes and move on."

"Is that all you're going to say?" I screeched, standing up abruptly from the chair. "Unbelievable!"

"Raven, you're out of pocket. I need you to calm down."

"I don't want to calm down because I—"

"Sit down...right now!" Dad raised his voice louder. Reluctantly, I eased back down into the chair in front of him.

"First of all, you will not come in here with that disrespect ever again. I won't have it." He pointed at me with a firm finger.

"I know I should've called before I came over but—"

"This isn't about you not calling, although you should've, but you gave your stepmother *the hand*!"

"Fine, I'll apologize to Veronica," I say haphazardly.

"You're out of line, Raven, and I need you to understand the boundaries here between parent and child. I'm your father." He pointed to himself. "And Veronica is your stepmother, whether you like it or not. You don't have to love her, but you will respect her as my wife."

I rolled my eyes to the ceiling.

"As for Taj, Adrian, or whomever else decided to be with someone else besides you, that's their loss. Trust me sweetheart, when you get to be my age, that high school stuff will be the least of your concerns," he said, like it was no big deal. "Regarding your mother and Gerald, kudos to them. They asked for your blessing the same way Veronica and I did as a courtesy, not because they *needed* your permission. I need you to stop having a two-year-old tantrum every time something doesn't go your way."

"I'm not having a tantrum, Dad, but I do have a right to be upset."

"Of course you do. I know it hurts to have breakups, and I know it hurts to see your mother and me with other people, but you're sixteen and it's time to grow up, Raven."

I could feel my eyes pooling with tears. "But I thought somehow there could still be a chance with you and mom."

"Listen"—he gestured firmly with his hands—"I will always love your mother for giving me a smart and beautiful daughter like you. Diane knows if there's anything she needs on your behalf, she can have it, but outside of that, we are never getting back together. That's a reality you need to accept."

"This is hard, Daddy," I admitted. As soon as I blinked, tears spilled down my cheeks.

"I understand." He softened his tone. "But if you love your mother and me, you should want us to be happy. Veronica and I have been married for three years now. She's tried to be your friend, and you have flat out given her a hard time. Today, I'm very disappointed in you. You crossed the line and went too far this time."

"I'm sorry, Dad."

He reached into his drawer and pulled out a piece of paper. He leaned over the desk, and that's when I realized he was handing me his credit card statement.

"The budget was three hundred. You spent seven."

"I'm sorry about that too."

"Raven, you need to show me you are. Until then, because of your disrespect and abuse of the freedoms we've given you, you are grounded. That means you don't get an allowance from me for two months. Hand me the credit card right now."

"But Daddy—"

"Nope, I don't want to hear it." He threw up his hand. "It's my fault for spoiling you this way, but it ends today. I need you to grow up."

I pouted as I reluctantly handed him his card back from my purse. "It's just that you and Mom never spend any time with me."

A wrinkle creased his forehead with concern.

"You may be right about that, but it's not an excuse for disrespect. I'll call your mother and discuss how we can do better. But in the meantime, let's go to the kitchen so you can apologize to Veronica. Perhaps you can stay for dinner afterwards and continue to smooth things over with her."

I dropped my head. Lamented, "Alright."

CHAPTER 24
TRUTH WHITE AS LILIES

LESLIE

Columbia, Temple, Spelman, and Howard had all accepted my application and gave me praise for the essay I had written about Champ, and for my high SAT scores. The acceptance letters also included offers for a full academic scholarship. It felt bittersweet, because as much as I wanted to go away to college, I knew I couldn't. I folded the letters and placed them back in the envelopes. I was about to drop them in a box with my pen pal letters when my phone rang.

"Hello?"

"Hi Leslie, how are you?"

"Oh, hi Aunt Naomi. I'm good."

"I hate to bother you at the last minute, but would you mind braiding Jasmine's hair?" she asked, sounding flustered. "I forgot I scheduled her to take school pictures on Monday, and Boogie can't do it. He's rehearsing for the school talent show."

"Sure. I'll ask Grandma. I'm sure she wouldn't mind."

After we said goodbye, I went downstairs and asked Grandma if it was OK for me to walk to Aunt Naomi's house around the corner from us.

"Just make sure you're back before the streetlights come on," Grandma said.

I was half-expecting to see Uncle Henry when I arrived at Aunt Naomi's house, but it was a reminder that he and Aunt Naomi had officially divorced. Jasmine ran into my arms as I leaned down for a hug. The smell of seasoned flour hung in the air, making my stomach growl.

"I'm cooking fried chicken and french fries if you'd like to stay for dinner," Aunt Naomi offered.

"I'd love to." My mouth was already watering for some of her famous buttermilk crispy chicken.

I sat down on the sofa, and Jasmine sat crisscross style on the floor between my legs while I cornrowed her hair in a cute style. *In Living Color* was playing on the living room TV. It was one of my favorites. By the time I finished fixing Jasmine's hair, Boogie came home from rehearsal. He greeted me with a quick hug and went and took a shower.

"Dinner is ready, guys," Aunt Naomi said, as she placed the food in the center of the dining room table an hour later.

Jasmine sprung up from the living room and ran into the dining room. Her colorful beads clicked with her movements.

"Am I pretty?" she asked her mom, coyly.

"Yes, you are." Aunt Naomi kissed her forehead and Jasmine climbed in the chair next to her.

Boogie walked into the dining room looking refreshed.

"Have a seat and say the prayer, then we can eat," Aunt Naomi said to him.

After dinner, Boogie took Jasmine upstairs to read her a bedtime story.

"Aunt Naomi, thank you for letting me write about Champ for my college admission process." I was helping her clean up the kitchen.

"You don't have to thank me. Champ was your cousin." She washed the dishes as I dried them.

"I got accepted to every college I applied to, and they're offering full scholarships."

"Congratulations! That's wonderful." A big smile stretched across her face.

"Thanks, but Grandma doesn't want me to go away to school. She told me to let Howard know that I'll be going there instead."

Aunt Naomi tilted her head. "Now, why would she tell you that?"

"She needs my help with taking care of Mama. Plus, no one knows where Lucci is and—"

"No, no, no, that's not right." Aunt Naomi shook her head. "I don't mean to cut you off, but that's just not right. Have you talked to your Aunt Diane about this?"

"Not yet."

"You know..." Aunt Naomi paused to choose her words carefully. "Diane and I have been telling your grandmother for years to give you more freedom."

"Really? I never knew that."

"They were private conversations on the phone, but Leslie you're eighteen," she said. "You have a right to decide which college you want to go to."

The thought of telling Grandma I wasn't going to attend Howard made my stomach turn in knots. I didn't want to disobey my grandmother, but my heart wanted me to make a decision that was different from hers. I continued to listen to Aunt Naomi, who always seemed to be a good voice of reason.

"Howard is a good school, but if you want to go away instead, I'll support you," Aunt Naomi assured me. "I just hate that your grandmother continues to hold you hostage the way she does your mother."

"What do you mean?" I asked, drying off the last dish.

"Don't get me wrong, I understood your grandmother's reasons at first, but through the years, I realized your mother deserved proper treatment, but your grandmother doesn't see it that way."

"Well, why not?"

"I honestly believe she's afraid Irene will start talking, and when she does, she'll probably confess that she was the one who killed the man who raped her, not your Uncle Donovan."

My jaw dropped. The plate slipped from my hand and crashed to the floor, shattering into pieces.

"Oh my gosh!" I gasped. "I'm-I'm-I'm sorry. I'll clean it up."

"It's okay. I'll get it." Aunt Naomi grabbed the broom and dustpan. My body shivered in shock from this news, as Auntie swept the broken pieces.

"Are you okay?" Aunt Naomi hugged me when she finished. My tongue felt glued to the roof of my mouth. I didn't know what to say. Aunt Naomi took me by the hand and led me to the living room. We sat down on the sofa together, as she grabbed the photo book from underneath the coffee table.

"Your grandmother promised she would tell you the truth once you were old enough to understand. By your reaction, I can tell she never did."

"She told me some of it, but I have always wanted to know more details." I wiped my sweaty palms on my pants.

Aunt Naomi opened the photo book. "It's going to be alright," she stroked my back with her free hand. "Let's start from the beginning."

As she started telling the story, and pointing out pictures, I visualized everything as if I were watching a movie.

"...and your Uncle Henry was the oldest," Aunt Naomi continued to tell the backstory. "He obeyed all the rules. He felt he had to do everything right since your grandfather was a strict disciplinarian and a Marine. And your grandma had high expectations for their education. She had never finished school, and only went as far as tenth grade after having Henry," Aunt Naomi explained, pointing out different family photos through the years. "Donovan was the youngest, and everyone said he was a rebel without a cause. Irene was next to the oldest. She was the smartest person in the family. She was so intelligent that she would do her parents' taxes by the time she was thirteen."

"Wow." I was in awe, and even more so, at the photos I'd never seen of Mama and her siblings when they were younger.

"Is this Uncle Henry's photo book?" I asked curiously.

"It is. He wants to keep it here for the children to see. Since you're family, I'm showing them to you too," she expressed gently.

Aunt Naomi continued. "Irene was the family favorite. Henry said their parents doted on her all the time and she could do no wrong. When I had met her, I felt she was really kind, but she was a little naïve socially."

"How so?" I asked, noticing Boogie walking back down the steps. He sat next to me on the sofa and listened in.

"If someone's car broke down, Irene loaned them hers. If there was a party, she brought the beer. People took advantage of her. Sad to say, even your Aunt Diane took advantage of her kindness sometimes. Henry said Diane would take Irene's car and return it without gas. She would wear her clothes without asking. She'd also leave Irene to do all the chores when they were younger. They had plenty of spats because of it, but it got heavy when Irene started dating Diane's ex-boyfriend, Evan. This is her and Evan right here." Aunt Naomi pointed to a handsome man with a light warm brown complexion and an Afro.

"And in this picture is your mom with Evan at a disco. And this other one is on Howard's campus. The duplicate of this photo is in your mother's room on the mirror. That's Evan's shadow. He took the picture."

"Diane was always bossing Evan around," Aunt Naomi continued. "She cheated on him with Raymond, Raven's dad, and then Evan broke up with her."

"Were they in high school?" Boogie asked.

"No, at the time, Irene was a senior in college, and Diane was a junior," she replied, flipping the pages. "Diane was always jealous of the attention Irene received from their parents, and even more since Evan and Irene had gotten engaged. Diane lied and told Irene she saw Evan kissing on another woman. Being the naïve person that Irene was, she believed Diane. But Diane could be a little convincing, I admit. She showed Irene a photo of Evan hugging the woman. Henry and I learned later from Evan that the woman was his African Studies professor. She had taken photos with all her students before traveling to Egypt, but Diane happened to see a photo of the professor hugging Evan, and made Irene believe there was more to it."

"Mmm-Umph! Aunt Diane was scandalous!" Boogie shook his head.

"Diane was trying to get into the Knight & McCormick Law Firm as an intern, and she knew that Percy Knight was the son of the owner and partner, who happened to have the biggest crush on Irene. Diane figured she could intern for the law firm if Percy and Irene had gotten together."

"Irene and Percy would run into each other at cabarets and discos from time to time, but since Irene was dating Evan, she always turned Percy down. Diane convinced Irene to go out with Percy to make Evan jealous. I told Irene that was childish, but she wouldn't listen. She trusted Diane and went out with Percy as payback to Evan."

Aunt Naomi flipped to another set of photographs in the book where we came across a beautiful picture of Mama. She was sitting in a round back straw chair wearing a red maxi dress and sandals, and Aunt Diane stood next to her wearing a red maxi dress, except hers had a floral pattern, and she wore high heels and a floppy hat to match. It looked like the photo was taken at a nightclub, and the photographer was by Mr. G., his signature was in the corner of the picture. To the far right, it looked like half the image of a man standing next to Aunt Diane.

"Who was that in the corner?" I pointed.

"That was Percy, your Uncle Henry cut him off the picture. That's as good as it got without losing Diane from the photo."

"What did he look like?" I asked, curiously.

"He was kind of short about 5'7 with a stocky build and wore glasses. Honestly, he looked like a harmless businessman on the outside. I think that was his deceptive tactic."

"My mom went out with him on one date?"

"Yeah," she sighed. "Just one date."

"Is that when...the assault...happened?" I asked, apprehensively. I was afraid of the answer, but I had to know the truth once and for all.

"Unfortunately, yes. Irene came home battered and bruised and told her parents that Percy...you know the rest." Aunt Naomi tried to say it tactfully. "Henry, who was a new police officer was determined to prove himself. He caught Percy right away and arrested him."

"The case went to trial, and Percy was found not guilty. We all felt the 'not guilty' verdict had to do with Percy's family political ties," Aunt Naomi explained. "It was a painful time for the family. So much so that your grandfather, Uncle Donovan, and Irene drove over to Percy's house seeking revenge. Henry said he and your grandmother were the only two in the family who didn't know the others had planned to do that."

"And then what?" I scooted to the edge of my seat in anticipation.

"Your grandfather and Uncle Donovan beat up Percy. When Irene saw that Percy was still alive and breathing, she shouted, 'Finish the job! Finish the job!' This is what Donovan, and your grandfather would later tell the family. When they refused, Irene snatched Percy's belt off his pants and choked him."

"WHAT?" Boogie and I were in shock.

"Yep, your grandfather and Donovan said something snapped inside of Irene. They tried to pull her off Percy, but the more they tugged her, the more she tightened her grip until Percy died. She spoke few words after that."

"Wow, Mama is a murderer?" I lamented, shaking my head.

"It sounds like Aunt Irene was a vigilante," Boogie stated.

"I'm not going to judge Irene for what she did," Aunt Naomi declared, and continued to tell the story. "The police never found the weapon because your grandfather told us he got rid of it. However, Percy's neighbor told police that she saw three people entering Percy's house. Based on her descriptions, the police brought in several people, including your Uncle Donovan who the neighbor identified in the lineup. However, your grandfather and your mom were never in the lineups because the police never viewed them as suspects."

"All this time I thought Uncle Donovan was locked up over something he did with Turk," I admitted.

"He did get locked up a few times over petty crimes he committed for Turk and Theresa, but not this time. He is innocent."

"Why didn't Aunt Irene go to jail since Uncle Donovan didn't do it?" Boogie asked, taking the words out of my mouth.

"Donovan took the fall for your Aunt Irene because he felt sorry for her. He said she would not have survived in prison," Aunt Naomi uttered somberly. "At any rate, when Donovan told the police he killed Percy, they asked who else was involved. Donovan stuck to his story and said it was just him, even though the neighbor said she saw three people. Ultimately, when they went to court, the judge felt Donovan was holding back further evidence, and because of his prior criminal history as well, he sentenced Donovan to thirty years in prison."

"Why would our grandparents allow their son to go to jail like that though?" Boogie asked. "That seems unfair."

"Diane told your grandparents that Donovan wouldn't get that much time since he pled guilty, but she wasn't experienced enough to know the law yet. Unfortunately, things didn't go as planned. Now Donovan is pleading his innocence. Hopefully, Gerald can help him with his appeal. Diane said there's a good chance he will get out since no weapon was ever found, and they only had one witness in the case. And that witness is deceased now."

"Will that mean Mama will go to jail if Uncle Donovan gets out?" I asked, nervously biting my nails.

"I'm not sure. I mean, she's mentally ill. Perhaps they can provide treatment for her, but I won't be

161

presumptuous." Aunt Naomi replied.

"I hope a judge shows mercy on Mama."

"We hope so too," Aunt Naomi and Boogie agreed.

"Quick question, did Grandpa really die in his sleep?" I asked, curiously.

"He did. When Irene managed to tell him that she was pregnant, and then Donovan was sentenced to thirty years in prison, it was all too much stress."

"I can see why. Man, that *is* a lot!" Boogie exclaimed.

"So, when exactly did my mother stop talking completely?" I wanted to know.

"When your grandfather died. She totally went into her shell and never spoke another word. Your grandmother had to raise you."

"Wow, I agree with Boogie, this *is* a lot." I rubbed the side of my temples.

"Now you know the *whole* truth." Aunt Naomi closed the photo album. "If anyone wants to know how you found out, they can come and ask me. I will tell them I felt you deserved to know."

"That's right, Mom, you tell them." Boogie snapped his finger and rolled his neck.

"Honey, go away to college and get your degree." Aunt Naomi hugged me. "Go and get yourself a life."

"Thank you so much, Auntie. I needed to know the truth."

She smiled. "Truth is white as lilies, and lilies represent a rebirth. Come on, let's get you home. It's getting late."

Aunt Naomi drove me home. Grandma asked how everyone was doing, and I gave her a short answer and went off to my room. I needed time to process everything. Even though Mama didn't go to prison like Uncle Donovan, her mind did. Just to think that all of this started with Aunt Diane. I needed to talk to Raven about this. I dialed her from my private phone.

"Raven, you're not going to believe this. I hope you're sitting down..."

CHAPTER 25
BIKE RIDING

MITCH

Leslie, Raven, Boogie, KC, Devante, and I rode our bikes to the Washington Monument. We were so tired by the time we reached the top of the hill that we fell out on the grass, spaced apart to give each other room, and caught our breath.

I lay back, with my hands behind my head and fingers intertwined, as I stared up at the monument. It looked like a postcard as its pointy tip seemed like it was kissing the blue sky. Leslie, who lay next to me, asked, "It's beautiful isn't it?"

"It is," I agreed, raising my brows toward my forehead. "Did you know Americans stole the structural style of the monument from the Egyptians, and that slaves helped to build it and the US Capitol?"

"I didn't, but it doesn't surprise me," she admitted. "How did you know that?"

"I read it. My mother always made sure I knew my history."

"When did your parents tell you that you were adopted?" she asked.

I started clapping my shoes together like windshield wipers. Sometimes heavy conversation made me antsy.

"I was about eight years old," I said. "A kid at school asked me why my skin looked darker than my parents. I never knew I was Black or White, to be honest. I just knew I was human."

Leslie took hold of my hand and entwined her fingers between mine.

"Have you ever met your real parents?"

"They're dead. They were both junkies," I replied, feeling more comfortable with her hands entwined with mine. "My biological mother, Lauren, left me at DC General Hospital after giving birth and never looked back. It was Katherine who reported her missing, and when no one came back to claim me, not even my biological father, Mitchell, she and John adopted me."

"I don't know how a mother could leave behind her own child."

"I didn't understand it either at first, but now I know they were sick and needed help."

"Do you know what they look like?"

"Yep." I lifted my hips so I could pull out my wallet from the pocket of my shorts. I handed Leslie a small, warped photo that my mom and dad took in a photo booth.

"You look like a combination of both, but you have your father's boyish eyes. Where did you get the picture?" Leslie stared at it like she was studying every detail.

"Lauren left it on the hospital bed. My mother said it seemed intentional, as if she wanted me to know who they were, at least."

"Thankfully, Mr. and Mrs. Larson took good care of you."

"My mom sure did. John Larson was a jerk. He never wanted me."

"Why? I bet you were a cute baby."

"I may have been cute, but John always felt because I was Black, I was an embarrassment."

"Don't say that."

"Well, that's how he felt. He got tired of me coming home from school complaining about being bullied. I was the only Black kid with White parents. They teased me for speaking properly, and for the activities I was into like rock climbing and skateboarding. I never fit in and got jumped every single day. When I was playing in Little League, and the other kids would go out for pizza after a winning game, they wouldn't invite John and me. John never stood up for me, he just put me on another team with Black kids, but I was still an outcast. After a while, John got tired of toting me around and explaining that I was adopted. He wanted kids of his own, but Katherine couldn't have any."

"I'm sorry to hear that."

"I'm not. Not for John, at least. He knocked up his secretary, and after that he and Katherine divorced."

"That's tough." Leslie nestled her head against my shoulder.

"I hated myself for it. Hearing Katherine cry every night, I felt like it was my fault, and so I started...you know."

"It's okay. You don't have to explain anymore." Leslie traced her fingertips over the scars on my wrists and raised her brow with concern. "But you're OK now, right?"

"Perfectly fine. Besides, the Navy wouldn't let me in if I wasn't mentally stable."

KC, Raven, Boogie, and Devante walked over to us.

"Hey, we're going inside the monument. You guys want to come?" KC offered.

"We're good. Probably going to grab a hot dog or something in a few." I rose from the grass and stretched the tension out of my arms and legs.

"Okay, we'll head over and catch up with you guys in a bit," KC said.

"Mitch, you and Leslie need to watch our bikes then," Raven interjected in a demanding tone.

"Would saying *please* be a stretch?" I puckered my brow.

Raven clucked her teeth. "Please."

"That's better."

"What*ever*," she rolled her eyes as she walked away.

"Just to think she probably could have had a chance with me if she wasn't so bourgeois and rude."

Leslie chuckled. "Oh yeah? I thought she would be too young for you."

"That too," I nodded. "I remember she used to leave love letters at my door."

Leslie stood up from the grass, dusted off her shorts. "Really? I never knew she did that."

"She'd include poems with her letters. They were kind of cute, but kiddie-like, so I'd toss them in the trash."

"I'm glad you didn't tell her you tossed them. It would've broken her heart."

"I never liked girls who were pressed for me. Besides, Raven's future is nothing short of tucking money between her hip and a thong."

Leslie smacked me on the back of the head.

"Ow!"

"Don't talk about my cousin like that."

"I was just joking around. I see you can be mean when you want to."

"Only when it comes to my cousins. Besides, if anybody is a freak, it's your ex-girlfriend, Angel."

I threw up my hands. "No argument there. She's had more passengers in that gate than an airline."

Leslie cracked up laughing.

"So, who are you taking to your prom?" I asked, skipping the subject. We'd been talking too much about our depressing family history. When she told me about her mom during our bike ride, I felt kind of sad.

"Why? Are you taking me?" her eyes lit up.

"Well, I mean, I don't see any other guys lining up outside your door."

"Oh hush." She playfully elbowed me. I tickled and wrestled her back down on the grass and pinned her arms down. I loved watching her laugh. Seeing her smile always made my day. I felt she deserved to be happy, and I planned to do my part by always making her smile.

CHAPTER 26
SURRENDER

LUCCI

Thankfully, Dre didn't die. I heard from Mitch, who had heard from his mom, a nurse, that Dre was making a slow recovery. Mitch had also loaned me forty dollars, but I needed sixty bucks to buy an Amtrak ticket to get out of dodge. I tried not to hang around my grandmother's old neighborhood too much out of fear that someone in my family may end up hurt because of me. But I needed money for food, and to get away.

Knowing it was the first of the month, I dipped into the crowded grocery store and stole a few snacks. I'd been couch-surfing between my girlfriends Keisha and Ling's houses. They got tired of me being around eating up all of their food and not helping to pay for anything. But when I was giving them money for Gucci bags and jewelry, they treated me like their king, even though they're a few years older than me. Now they kicked me out on the streets. I had no choice but to go to my mother's house.

The front door to my mother's house was open, but the screen was locked, and I could see inside the house. I watched as a woman wearing a purple dress with a matching hat and shoes approach the door.

"Boy, I thought you were a homeless person."

"Ma?" I gawked.

"I thought you would have been locked up by now or shot dead," she spat, unlocking the screen door to let me in.

By her looks I didn't recognize her, but when she opened her ghetto ratchet mouth, I did. Mom looked good. Her skin was clear, she'd put on a few pounds, and her hair was done nicely.

I dropped my big black plastic trash bag filled with clothes on the living room floor. My so-called girlfriends wouldn't even hold my stuff for me.

"You know the cops are looking for you."

"I know," I said, opening the fridge. It was empty except for a small jug of water. No surprises there. I grabbed it. Guzzled it down. Toting my bag around in the muggy heat made me thirsty.

"Where are you going?" I asked, walking back into the living room, noticing a small suitcase by her feet.

"I'm going to live my best life. Something I should have done a long time ago."

"Where?"

"A place where I can soak in the sun."

"So, wait, you were just going to leave me?"

"What else was I supposed to do?"

"Be a mother and find out what was going to happen to me!"

"Child, you know good and well I ain't never been much of a mother to you," she said bitterly, withdrawing a cigarette from her purse. "Besides, the faster I can get out of DC, the better. It's too much temptation here for me."

"What about this house? You're just going to leave it?"

"It was never mine. The government owns it."

My eyes looked up at the dusty framed photo of the two of us on the wall. She had replaced the frame when it broke after Earl threw me into it years ago, but we were never the family that was smiling in the picture.

"Where did you get the money to leave town?" I had an itchy feeling something else was up. Being on the streets, you learn people, and I knew my mother didn't have enough money to leave out of town.

"Why are you worried about it?" She sneered.

"Turk gave you some money, right? I know he paid you. How much did he give you to leave town? And why?"

"Two bricks," she said, then she exhaled smoke through her nostrils. I knew two bricks was twenty-thousand dollars. "He's turning this house into a trap house. He always wanted it that way, so I'm leaving. He can have it."

"I want some of it."

She blurted out a loud, wicked laugh. "Negro, are you stupid or dumb? I'm not giving you a dime."

"I need to leave town too before they kill me. Come on Ma, I'm your son, and Turk is my cousin. We're supposed to be family."

"Turk ain't never been our blood family."

"Say what?"

"Look boy, hand me that ashtray from the windowsill. I'll tell you in a minute."

I grabbed the ashtray, but I didn't like the way she was talking to me. I never did.

She tapped the ashes in the tray before she spoke again, then placed it on the table in front of her.

"Turk is not your cousin. He was my pimp, and his mama was the Madam."

"WHAT!"

"My mother was a drunk who beat the crap out of me all the time, but Turk's mother, Gloria, was the neighbor who would look after me. She ran a brothel next door until the cops shut her down, then she moved down here to DC. A few years later, she wrote me a letter and included a bus ticket for me to come here. I left New York and I never looked back," she explained in a casual tone.

"Then what?" I asked, curiously.

"When Glo died, Turk took over. He wasn't good at the pimp game, but we did what we needed to do to pay the bills. See that picture over there with Aunt Glo, Turk, and me standing with those women on the steps?" She pointed, and I looked over my shoulder.

"That was a brothel Aunt Glo ran uptown."

"Wow, all this time, I thought they were just your friends."

"They were at the time, but when the cops raided our house and took it, they scattered like roaches. Ain't no real friends in this world, boy."

"You got that right," I said, thinking of Dre and how he betrayed me and took out my homies. And Peanut who smashed Marcia behind my back.

"Turk started dealing drugs, and we met your daddy. He was our hitman, but he wanted to get in the game. Turk wouldn't put him on, but he met somebody else bigger than Turk and started making more money than us. Yeah, he was big time," she said, wincing her eyes against the cigarette smoke. "I slept with him so I could figure out who his connection was but ended up pregnant with you. By the time I told him I was pregnant, he was headed to prison for what happened to your Aunt Irene."

"What did he have to do with that?"

"He took the heat for what she did."

"Wait a minute." I shook my head, confused.

"Your Aunt Irene choked out the guy who raped her. Served him right." She laughed like a wicked witch.

I didn't have a lot of time to think about all of what my mother was telling me. I needed to get to the point so I could jet before people knew where I was.

"Give me some of that money!" I snatched her purse from her lap the way I would snatch it violently from people I had robbed in the streets.

"Fool, you can have that purse. You think I'm stupid enough to ride around town with that kind of bread? Turk wired the money to my account. It's safer that way."

"You owe me."

"I gave you life. That was enough." She eased out of the chair and grabbed her suitcase. "I think that's my taxi tooting the horn." I wanted to kick her in the back on the way out, but I couldn't bring myself to do it. She was still my mother.

"If you know what's good for you, Lucci, turn yourself

in," she said, and then she walked out the door.

The phone rang, distracting my thoughts, but I let it ring a few times before I picked it up. I didn't say anything as I held the phone to my ear. I wanted to make sure of who was on the other end before I spoke.

"Hello? Hello? Is someone there?" I recognized Aunt Diane's voice on the other end. "Lucci, if this is you, please don't hang up."

"It's me, Aunt Di."

"We have been looking all over for you!" Aunt Diane's voice sounded panicked. "I can't let another person in this family go to jail. Stay right there and we'll go to the police."

"Nah. I ain't trying to go to jail."

"Everything will work out just fine. Do you trust me?"

I had a flashback of the time she'd stood up for me as a kid when Earl had beaten me.

"Yeah, I do."

"Stay right there and don't leave. Gerald and I are coming to get you right now. Gerald is a criminal lawyer, and he will help you the same way he is helping with your father's appeal."

"Folks out there think I killed Mook and Peanut, but I didn't. Dre did."

"We know you didn't do it."

"How?"

"A Latino man who was part of that drug deal had been in police custody. Henry said the cops offered him a deal if he gave information about the shooters. He identified Dre in the photos they showed to him, and said he was the one who shot your friends. But you still need to turn yourself in *today* and tell the cops you acted in self-defense."

"Alright, but ya'll need to hurry up before folks find out where I am, including the cops."

She heaved a sigh of relief. "We're on our way. If the cops show up before we get there, ask for a lawyer. Don't say anything else no matter what happens. Ask for a lawyer and only talk to Gerald."

"I got it."

CHAPTER 27
DEAR DIARY

LESLIE

June 17, 1990

Dear Diary,

I'm a high school graduate! I graduated with honors as a valedictorian. I never felt so happy and scared at the same time. I was happy to have finished high school and achieved so much but scared on the other hand about my future. I wrote back to the college of my choice, and I told them I accept the scholarship offer, but I still haven't told Grandma that I'm not going to Howard. With everything that has been going on with Lucci, I'm still trying to find the right moment.

In more good news, I lost 40 pounds from all the bike riding and long walks with Mitch. I feel lighter and I can breathe so much better. I haven't needed my inhaler in over a month! Losing weight helped me to look nicer in my pretty lavender prom dress. Mitch took me to my senior prom, and we had an amazing time! He was the perfect gentleman. I know if Champ were here, he would be surprised that Mitch and I are a couple. Although I'm not sure for how long since Mitch is leaving the end of next month for the Navy.

Ms. Larson invited me to go shopping with her yesterday for her wedding dress, and when we were on the way to the mall, we saw Angel and her sisters getting arrested by the police. It looked like they had raided

Angel's house. Ms. Larson said to me, "I'm glad the cops responded to my calls of concern. I told them there were suspicious activities at that location," and she winked at me. I couldn't help but laugh. Even though I never liked to see anyone get into trouble, Angel was reaping what she had sown. None of us felt bad for what happened to her, but we did feel for Lucci.

Lucci confessed everything to the cops who sent police divers to retrieve his gun from the Potomac River. The ballistics did not match the bullets that killed Mook and Peanut, but the bullets from Dre's gun did. Therefore, Dre was sentenced to life in prison while Lucci was sentenced to two years at a bootcamp detention center in Ohio for troubled teens. He was charged with attempted robbery and having an unregistered firearm. He must also pay a $2500 fine by the time he turns 21 and perform 500 hours of community service. I hated that Lucci had to go away, but a part of me felt it was for his own good. Uncle Donovan tried to warn Lucci that the street life would cost him his life or time in jail.

Speaking of Uncle Donovan, a judge denied his appeal since he used to be a known hitman. The judge didn't believe that an honor student like Mama, who had never gotten into any trouble would do such a thing. However, because of Uncle Donovan's changed behavior while in prison, he did agree to reduce his sentence to twenty-five years instead of thirty. That means he'll be home by the year 2000.

Well, I need to run. We're going to see Boogie in a talent show at Hine this evening. He's been practicing for several weeks now. We can't wait to see him perform!

Until later...

-Leslie

CHAPTER 28
A POCKET FULL OF TEARS

BOOGIE

On stage is where I felt alive. Me and my dance crew, the Rhythm Rock Boys, had to change our routine from C+C Music Factory because Nicole gave us a heads up that someone else was going to dance to the song and try to upstage us. Instead, we selected a hip-hop dance routine to Black Sheep's "The Choice is Yours." We brought the house down! We won the school talent contest and did so well that a talent scout gave my mother a business card to audition for *Showtime at the Apollo* in New York. We were beyond excited.

"I'm so proud of you!" Mom hugged me after the show. "You guys did an amazing job."

"Thank you."

"Boogie was dancing like this." Jasmine tried to imitate my dance moves by twirling around in circles. Her long, colorful braids swung around like a carousel. I picked her up and kissed her cheek.

"That was a dope performance, Boogie!" Mitch approached me and shook my hand.

"Thanks bro."

"I can see you in music videos already. You'll probably end up dancing for MC Hammer or Heavy D. & the Boyz." Raven stepped in and hugged me.

"Aw, I love you for saying that, Cuz." I said, just as my mother snapped a Polaroid picture of us.

"Boogie, you're the best dancer in the family, so don't ever drop the name we gave you." Leslie squeezed me with her motherly embrace.

"This means a lot coming from you, my eldest sister-cousin," I winked.

"We need to get going or we will be late," Raven mentioned to Leslie and Mitch.

"Where are y'all going?" I asked.

"To see the movie *Pretty Woman.*"

"Oh, where's Adrian? Did he go get the car or something?" I looked around, assuming it was a double date.

"No. We're no longer friends, but like my dad said it's his loss." She flipped her hair.

"I told you to quit dogging him out," I shook my head.

"What-*ever*. We'll see you later," Raven said, walking off with Mitch and Leslie.

I felt someone tap my shoulder and I turned around.

"Hey Boogie." Nicole's pretty face smiled, as she wrapped her arms around me. "You were awesome tonight!"

"Thank you."

She smelled nice and felt so soft and warm in my arms. *Is my body betraying me? Why am I so turned on by this...girl?*

"We're going skating Saturday night if you want to bring your dance crew to meet me and my friends," she offered.

"Uhm...sure, I guess that should be cool." I said, feeling a little taken aback by the invitation. *She can't tell I'm gay...or am I?* I liked how warm she felt in my arms, and I felt a strong desire to grab both of her breasts and squeeze them. I was curious and wanted to know if they felt soft like a balloon.

"Cool. We'll see you at Crystal's Skating Rink," she smiled flirtatiously as she walked away with her friends.

"Cute girl. You guys look good together," Mom handed me the Polaroid picture that she snapped of us.

I eyed the photo, feeling so mesmerized by her beauty that I didn't notice my father approaching us until I handed mom the picture back.

A few lingering guests in the auditorium stared at him, wondering why he was there. I always hated how uncomfortable people's faces looked when a police officer like my dad appeared on the scene. I think he got a kick out of intimidating others when he was in uniform. He must've just gotten off work.

"Nolan, great show." Dad spoke without so much as a grin to show that he meant it. If *suck the air out the room* had a face, his was it.

"What-*ever*," I rolled my eyes. Took my sister Jasmine's hand and walked out of the auditorium.

Mom invited Dad to have dinner with us after the talent show. She had already prepared the meal, and they were making small talk in the kitchen while she was warming it up. Jasmine and I watched an episode of *A Different World* in the living room. I immediately thought of Nicole, who favored Jasmine Guy, except Nicole was much younger. I kept recalling how she felt in my arms when she hugged me. My feelings grew stronger than I had ever experienced before.

I tried to think of something else, like the Rhythm Rock Boys dance crew. They wanted me to join them at Tracks for Teen Night this Saturday. The nightclub has a special night for gay teenagers one Saturday a month, and I hadn't gone out dancing in a while since I was busy practicing for the talent show. I'm still glad we won. But the thought of hanging out with my crew suddenly didn't feel as exciting as being with Nicole.

I was confused. *Am I bisexual? Why am I having these strong feelings about Nicole if I'm gay?*

Maybe I will go skating with Nicole this Saturday just to see if I still feel the same way I'm feeling right now. Just as I picked up the phone to call my dance crew to tell them I wouldn't be going to Tracks, a news alert came across the TV and grabbed my full attention.

"We are interrupting this program with a special newsbreak. Police performed the biggest drug raid in the history of DC moments ago. Police arrested close to a hundred people as part of an operation called "The Big Sting." Among those arrested were notorious drug lord Tyrone Timothy Jakes, who is also known as "Turk." Upon hearing about the shakedown, Jakes attempted to board a plane that was headed to Mexico when he was met by federal agents. Jakes has been charged with numerous federal violations, including operating a criminal enterprise, drug trafficking with a conspiracy to distribute, and racketeering. If convicted, Jakes and several of his co-conspirators could face life in prison."

"Mom, Dad, come quick, it's Turk on the TV!" I shouted.

They rushed into the living room. TV cameras and news reporters pushed their microphones toward Turk's face, seeking a statement as police officers led him and his crew into the back of a white police van.

"They finally got him!" Dad clapped. "The sting worked."

"Unbelievable." Mom shook her head. "I thought the police would never catch him."

"All these years, Turk and his crew have been selling that poison in our community and killing our people. I hope they never see the light of day. If you guys knew how many crack babies came into this world from their dope dealing, you would feel relieved the way I do right now," Dad declared, beaming a smile so big you would have thought he'd won the lottery. I hadn't seen my father smile like this since Champ used to win basketball games.

"It's about time, I'm going to call Diane and tell her the news." Mom took the cordless phone with her into the kitchen.

Dad sat opposite me on the sofa. Jasmine had fallen asleep on my lap. Dad started talking about The Big Sting operation, and how the FBI had finally decided to put together a task force two years ago in '88 when crack cocaine had completely taken over our city.

"I witnessed many honest-working people fall into the traps of drugs over the years, but crack was the worse drug I had ever seen during the 80s. It didn't matter if you were Black, White, Hispanic or any other race. I saw firsthand how crack turned all kinds of people into zombies right before my eyes. With Turk and his drug runners off the streets, I hope DC will get back to being a safe place to live again." Dad's eyes lit up.

Even though I never liked small talk with Dad, what he was saying about our city made sense.

"Okay, guys, dinner is warmed up. Let's eat," Mom called us to the table.

We ate dinner, and Mom and Dad did most of the talking while I thought about what type of dance routine my crew and I could perform for the audition for *Showtime at the Apollo*. Mom shared the talent scout's business card with Dad.

"Sam Shutters, huh?" Dad grinned and tucked the card in the pocket of his shirt. "I'll give him a call and make sure he's legit. I can't have him taking advantage of my son." He winked at me.

I found his gesture out of character and weird. Maybe he was still riding the high regarding the news of Turk going to jail.

"I don't know if you've heard, but Diane told me she's pregnant," Mom mentioned to Dad, but it was news to me as well.

"I bet Raven is just thrilled," Dad mocked in a sarcastic tone.

Mom chuckled. "I don't think so. She went to live with her father, but you know that only lasted a week. She went back home and told Diane that Veronica and the twins got on her nerves."

"Raven has always been spoiled. They need to give her more attention. Speaking of which, I think Boogie and Jasmine could use more of my attention as well."

Mom blushed. "I'm happy to hear you say that, Henry,

and I'm glad to see you sober. I'll leave you and Boogie alone to talk." She collected our plates when we finished.

Dad cleared his throat. "Boogie."

I looked up briefly and then lowered my eyes. *Why is he calling me Boogie now?*

"I'm sorry."

"Sorry for what?" I mumbled with my chin tucked down.

"I'm apologizing for everything, son." Dad stood up from the table, and when he walked over to me and stretched out his hand, I flinched.

"I'm not...I'm not going to hit you, Boogie." His eyebrows jumped. He was startled by my reaction.

"I love you and I promise I won't ever hit you again." Dad wrapped his arms around me, and I cringed. It felt like a stranger's touch. This wasn't supposed to be happening.

"Please let me go."

"I feel bad about the things I said and did to you, son. I treated you like nothing because that's how I felt after your brother died."

"I don't want to hear this, please let me go!"

Dad's arms eased off me, and I walked into the living room, but he wouldn't give up.

"Boogie, Champ is gone now. It's something I realize I must accept." Dad sat next to me. "Therapy helped me to realize that I still have one more son to raise."

"You're just saying that because you want Mom back."

"No, son. Your mother made it clear that we're never getting back together," he said, voice lowering in disappointment as he twiddled his thumbs. "But I'm still your father, and I know you need me in your life."

Who is this person? Did you swallow my dad?

"Truth is..." he paused and took a deep breath. "I need you too, buddy."

"But I'm not Champ."

"I never wanted you to be. It was wrong for me to compare you to him."

"All I ever did was try to make you happy, but nothing I

did could ever earn me the same attention that you gave to Champ."

He exhaled deeply. "You're right, but you have my full attention now, so just be yourself."

"What if I don't know who I really am yet?" I choked, wiping a small tear that escaped my eye. "Are you going to beat me while I try to figure things out?"

"No, I won't do that." He wrapped his arm around me and scooted close to me. This time I didn't flinch, but the tears streamed.

"I shouldn't cry like this, right? Crying is for sissies. That's what Champ used to say."

"No, crying is being human. Champ had it wrong," he admitted. "I love you son."

"I love you too, Dad."

"From now on, I want us to communicate openly with each other and with respect, even if we don't agree."

"Okay."

"Some buddies of mine are taking their sons on a fishing trip next week, but if you don't want to go, I will understand."

"I've never been fishing before."

"Good, then it's settled." Dad stood up from the sofa. "I'll pick you up next week."

"Dad, wait!" I called just as he turned the doorknob.

He turned around. "What is it, son?"

I shoved my hands in my pocket. Tried to piece together the words in my mind that matched what I felt in my heart.

"I need some advice. You see, there's this girl named Nicole..."

CHAPTER 29
ELEPHANT IN THE ROOM

RAVEN

Mom and I were planning a surprise graduation party for Leslie, making a list of items to buy from the store, when she suddenly threw up all over the kitchen counter. It seemed like every day Mom was getting sick from something she ate, or the slightest smell would send her hurling to the pearly white commode. She claimed her doctor said this was all normal, but I was sick and tired of cleaning up puke. I tried living with my dad for a while, but their house was too busy with the twins, so I moved back home.

"I'll grab the bleach," Gerald said, opening the cleaning supply cabinet we had created under the kitchen sink for easy access.

"No, Gerald, don't put bleach on my granite countertops!" Mom protested, as she peeped her head from the guest bathroom that she had run into to purge. Gerald grabbed a softer cleaning agent instead.

"I think you and I may have to do the planning for your cousin's surprise graduation party," Gerald said to me.

"I can do it. I'll call Leslie's friend KC. She's been wanting to check out the new St. Charles Towne Center down here anyway."

"Are you sure?" Gerald puckered his thick brow that sprouted strands of gray.

"Positive."

"Okay then. Here's my card. Buy whatever is needed but keep it under $200, will you?"

I quickly took his credit card and smiled. "Will do."

Gerald went to see if Mom was OK in the bathroom, I called KC and asked her to meet me at St. Charles in an hour. I wanted to give her enough time to drive down from DC. I headed upstairs to freshen up.

As I was combing my long wavy hair before the mirror on my dresser, I noticed an ugly pimple near my nose. I instantly panicked. I couldn't possibly be seen with a booger-looking pimple on my face. Pimples were always a sign I was about to start my period or was dealing with too much stress. I leaned in close to the mirror and popped it with my fingernail when my mother walked in.

"Rave, you got a second?" she asked.

"What's up?" I put on concealer and foundation to hide the pimple.

Mom sat down on my bed, crossing one plump leg over the other. I never want to become pregnant if it means gaining weight and being sick all the time like Mom.

"I think it's time we discuss the elephant in the room, don't you?" she asked, tilting her head. Her face had a nice glow, but her nose was spreading across her face like a rhino.

I looked at the Cartier watch on my wrist—a gift from my father for missing his last weekend visit with me. He decided to go to Florida for a mini vacation with his buddies. He'd won the big case he was working on. Said he needed a break. The watch was diamond-gorgeous, but I'd much rather be with him any day.

"Guess I can spare a few minutes," I shrugged.

"It's time to discuss you and Gerald, especially with our wedding coming up in a few months."

I heaved a sigh that blew my bangs off my forehead. "Look, if you want to marry Gerald, it really doesn't matter to me anymore."

"Then why do you always look hurt when we bring up

the subject?" she questioned. "And please be honest."

"Fine," I turned from the mirror and sat next to her. "Since we're being honest, I feel like you've only been there for me in spurts. You and Dad buy me whatever I want just to get out of your hair, and Gerald is already doing the same thing. When the baby comes, I'll probably be invisible."

She huffed in shock. "Raven, you never wanted to be around us, so don't even try it."

"Yes, I did, Mom!" I bellowed out. "Dad promised to get us together, but he never did."

"Our schedules conflicted."

"Right, it's always about work."

"You're exaggerating, Raven," she laughed sarcastically.

"Why are we having this discussion if you're not going to take me seriously and deny everything I'm saying?"

"I think your viewpoint is a little off, sweetie."

"OK, that's it!" I threw up my hands. "I'm going to meet up with KC."

"Raven, wait!"

"Mom, I need to go."

"We need to continue this conversation," she insisted. "Please...sit down," she tapped her hand on the bed.

I flopped back down. Crossed my arms.

"Your dad and I have to work and that's non-negotiable. When you become a parent and a homeowner, you will see what I mean."

"Why is there always an excuse for what you do? You're always justifying or denying. Just like you're in denial of the fact that Aunt Irene wouldn't have been raped by Percy Knight had you not set them up on a date," I blurted out every subject that had built up in me.

Her mouth dropped. "Excuse me? Who told you that?"

"Does it matter?"

Mom's glowing look turned into a shudder of surprise. Her eyes looked bewildered as if she was trying to find a comeback line to say.

"That's why I don't like talking to you about how I feel,

because you always find a way to make me feel guilty about my own feelings. You hurt people, Mom, and you hurt Aunt Irene, and now she doesn't even talk."

"Are you finished?"

"I'm done."

"Good. For the record, I don't like hurting people. Yes, I set her up with Percy, but I never knew he was a rapist. I love my sister and would never be that cruel to her," she expressed with so much emotion that I believed her this time.

"Percy was kind, well-mannered, and smart. At times, a little snarky, but I never knew his history with violating women until some other women came forward years later," her voice cracked and her eyes watered. "I hate what happened to Irene. Every day I wish I could take it all back. Every time I go into that courtroom and defend my clients in a sexual harassment case, I go for the jugular vein."

"What does that have to do with *our* relationship?"

"I'm explaining to you my regret over what happened in the past since you decided to throw it in my face." She shook her head in frustration. "Look, just stick to the point here and tell me how we can fix our relationship."

"You're the parent. Figure it out."

"Now see, that right there!" She pointed. "That's not going to work. Your smart mouth and teeth clucking and eye rolling needs to stop."

"I get it from you."

Mom buried her face in her hands. "Ugh! I can't win with you." She jumped up abruptly and began to pace the room. "Look Raven, your father and I are not perfect, but we are doing the best we can. Gerald and Veronica are too."

I felt like our conversation was going in circles with neither of us wanting to give in.

"I never expected you guys to be perfect. Just wanted your time with me to be non-negotiable."

"Fair enough," she flipped up her hand. "We'll try harder to find a balance but we're going to need your patience and mutual respect. Can you meet us halfway?"

I bobbed my head. "I think I can."

She grinned. Took my hand and squeezed it. "I'd love it if you tried."

CHAPTER 30
SET ME FREE

LESLIE

I was hot curling Mama's hair in her room while the TV played an episode of *Blossom*.

"All done. Would you like some lipstick so you can look pretty?" I asked, grabbing the small makeup kit from the dresser. Mama's eyes crinkled at the corners. She sat still and allowed me to put lipstick on her lips. When she smiled, I knew she liked it.

"Mama, just because you can't talk doesn't mean you don't deserve to feel like a woman."

I walked her over to the mirror on her dresser so she could see how pretty I made her look. Her long hair draped her shoulders, and she had on just a little bit of makeup. A big, toothy smile spread across her face.

"You look beautiful, Mama. I love you."

Suddenly, her bedroom door swung open.

"What the heck is this?" Grandma barged into the room, holding up a letter in her hand.

I shrugged, set the lipstick down on the dresser, and said, "I don't know."

"Little girl, don't you play with me. You know *exactly* what this is. You told me you were going to Howard University."

"Well, I—"

"*Dear Leslie, welcome to our Columbia University family! We thank you for your letter of intent. As a proud scholar of a four-year merit academic scholarship, our journalism department is happy to have you this coming*

August..." she read. "You told these people you're going to their university without discussing this with me?"

Grandma was so loud she drowned out the TV. For a little woman, she could be as loud as a Chihuahua.

"I was planning to talk to you about it but—"

"What the heck you mean you were planning on talking to me about it? You have already made the decision according to this letter, and they're giving you a scholarship."

"You're right, I have made the decision to go to Columbia," I said, trying to keep up my confidence the way Champ had always said to stand up for myself, and Lucci too.

"Over my dead body!" Grandma ripped the letter straight down the middle.

"But Grandma—"

"You are not going away to college, and that's final."

"Why not?"

"Your mother needs you, Leslie."

"But what about what I need?"

"You're just a child. You don't know what you need."

"I'm not a child, and I'm going to Columbia whether you—ow!"

Grandma cut me off with a harsh slap across the cheek.

"Oh my gosh, child, look what you done made me do," Grandma cried. "I...I'm sorry..."

She rushed out of the room, and when I heard the door slam and lock, I knew she'd gone into the bathroom.

I rubbed the sting out my cheek and stood there a moment, trying to understand what had just happened when Mama stormed out of the room.

"Mama, where are you going?" I ran behind her. She rushed down the hall to the bathroom and pounded on the door with her fist. I'd never seen her react this way before. It was a new behavior. Rage filled her eyes and her nostrils flared as she pounded on the bathroom door like a madwoman.

"I will be out in a minute!" Grandma yelled. We heard the toilet flush, followed by the water running in the sink. Grandma swung open the door.

"What is going on?" Grandma held the cigarette she'd been smoking in her hand. "Irene, go on back in the room. Don't stand here looking at me like that. Your daughter had no business disrespecting me that way."

Mama's eyes were fixed on Grandma like the target of a laser.

"Go on back to your room and be a good girl now." Grandma pointed with her cigarette wedged between her two fingers. "Besides, we all know what happened the last time you lost your temper. We don't need another person going to prison for your behavior."

Grandma's words struck a chord with Mama. She belted out a loud grunt that sounded like a beast, and next thing I knew, she had her hands around Grandma's throat.

"No Mama, don't do that!" As I pulled Mama back, Grandma's hands flung backward, sending her cigarette flying.

WHOOOSH

The bathroom curtains immediately lit up in flames.

CHAPTER 31
UP IN SMOKE

MITCH

"Mitch! MITCH! Come quick," Mom shouted from downstairs.

I was about to take a shower because I had just come from Watkins playground shooting hoops with Adrian and Devante.

I rushed downstairs, still wearing sweaty shorts and a T-shirt.

"What's wrong, Mom?"

"The Walkers' house is on fire!" she said, holding the phone to her ear. "I can't believe 911 has me on hold."

I opened the door. Orange flames burst through the top-level windows of the house. I ran across the street.

"I called 911, but the line was busy," Ms. Jean, the neighbor said, as she stood out on her front porch with a paranoid look on her face.

Other neighbors stood outside, watching the flames and unsure of what else to do. All I could think about was Leslie, and my heart pounded with fear.

"HELP! HELP!" I could hear Leslie and her grandmother screaming from inside. We couldn't just stand around and do nothing while waiting for the fire department. I kicked the living room window until it shattered enough for me to crawl inside.

"LESLIE! LESLIE!" I called out as I ran upstairs.

About halfway, I could see the hallway was smoking and in flames, so I ran back down the stairs and to the back of the house. Leslie's bedroom faced the back.

"Mitch, we're up here!" Leslie shouted, and when I looked up, she was standing in the window with her mother and grandmother next to her. They all looked afraid.

"Leslie! Jump!"

She looked petrified. I could see nothing but smoke behind them, and she started to cough uncontrollably.

"Mitch, it's too high for her to jump!" her grandmother shouted in a panic.

I remembered there was a ladder in their shed, and I ran inside. It was dark, and when I tried to pull the string to turn the light, it broke, so I had to feel my way around for it.

"HURRY MITCH! MY BEDROOM DOOR IS IN FLAMES!" Leslie shouted louder, making my hands tremble with fear.

As I felt my way around the shed, I touched what felt like a piece of plywood, and I used it to prop the shed door open. It was just enough light for me to see the ladder propped against the wall. I grabbed it and ran out. I placed the ladder against the house, but the top was about ten feet lower than the window.

"Leslie, you're going to have to slide down at least halfway before you can reach the ladder."

"I can't!" she cried, followed by a loud cough as thick smoke floated behind her.

"Yes, you can! You don't have a choice. Save yourself for once."

Suddenly, Leslie's mother pushed her out the window.

"NO!" I panicked, but as Leslie came tumbling down, I caught her in my arms. My knees buckled a little, but I caught her.

"Oh my God!" Leslie panted out of breath, holding her hands over her heart.

"Are you okay?"

"I need my...inhaler." She wheezed.

"Help me!" Mrs. Walker shouted, then she turned around and climbed out of the window. I ran over just in time as she slid down. Her foot hit the ladder awkwardly, knocking it to the ground. As she tumbled, I caught her in my arms for a safe landing.

"Mitch!" Mom called, rushing to the backyard gate. I heard sirens, indicating that the firetrucks were nearby.

"Mama, please jump!" Leslie squealed, sounding short of breath.

The firetruck pulled up and firefighters cleared the way of onlookers standing by and observing the scene. They rushed toward the house with their long firehose and a ladder.

The firefighter climbed his much taller ladder, but when he reached for Irene, she flinched.

"Mama, it's OK. He's there to save you!" Leslie wheezed.

"Please get her some oxygen. I'll coach her mother down," I said to the paramedics, who also came rushing to the scene.

"You can do it, Ms. Irene! Let them help you," I shouted.

As if she understood my familiar voice, she let the firefighter grab her and pull her down, just when a ball of fire burst into the room. Firefighters turned on the water hose after we told them no one else was inside. They put out the fire to keep it from spreading through the whole house.

After taking deep puffs of air from the oxygen mask, Leslie walked over and collapsed in my arms.

"Thank you so much for saving us, Mitch."

"I couldn't lose another Walker."

"Mitch, you're a blessing, sugar," Mrs. Walker gasped, as paramedics gently placed her and Irene on the emergency stretchers. "You saved our lives." The paramedics gave them oxygen masks and rolled them to the ambulance.

I never felt so relieved in all my life.

"Champ would've been proud of you, Mitch," Leslie stated. Her head was nestled against my chest.

"Yeah, he would've been."

CHAPTER 32
THROUGH THE FIRE

LESLIE

July 10, 1990

Dear Diary,

I'm truly thankful to God that He helped Mitch save our lives. The Washington Post wrote a nice piece about him rescuing us, and Mayor Marion Barry awarded him with a Life Saving Medal. I kept the newspaper article as a souvenir. I'm going to miss him when he leaves later this month.

Aunt Naomi helped me to get new copies of my high school diploma and my honorary awards since she works for DC Public Schools. Thankfully, she and Aunt Diane had taken photos during my graduation or else I wouldn't have any senior pictures. And Mitch's mom was nice enough to make copies of the photos that Mitch and I had taken during my senior prom. Aunt Diane helped replace my clothes, and Aunt Naomi's mother donated clothes to Grandma and Mama.

Unfortunately, my old diary is gone forever. It was my most valued personal belonging. I had kept the diary since I was nine years old. I'm writing this entry in a brand-new diary that Raven bought for me. It has a leather cover and gold trimming around the pages. She said, "I know how much you love to write, and I promise not to read this one this time."

Grandma and I are living with Aunt Naomi, and Mama

is back at St. Elizabeth Hospital. The doctors at St. Elizabeth diagnosed Mama with Adult Selective Mutism caused by Post Traumatic Stress Disorder (PTSD). The fire wouldn't have ever happened if I had the courage to tell Grandma the truth. I've been blaming myself ever since.

-Leslie

Sunday Morning Service

"...and sometimes your own family can hold you emotionally hostage," Pastor Ryan was preaching. "You see, they always seem to have a lot of emergencies, and you may find yourself running to their rescue either by physically helping them, financially bailing them out of trouble, or doing other favors for them, but that can be emotionally draining to your spirit. When you are emotionally drained in your spirit, you won't have any energy left for yourself or the God you serve."

After the sermon, a lightbulb went off in my head, as if God was talking to me and giving me the answers I'd been hoping for. Although Grandma and I had talked about Mama and her situation, we never talked about what happened that day of the fire, namely me going away to college. I needed to find the courage to have a heart-to-heart talk with Grandma. I would be leaving for college next month, and I needed to make sure she was going to be fine with me going away.

After Sunday dinner, I joined Grandma in the living room. She was sitting on the sofa knitting a pair of blue booties for Aunt Diane, who learned she was having a boy. *Family Matters* was playing on the TV. Grandma loved the Steve Urkel character, and occasionally she would look up and crack up laughing, but I could tell by her countenance most days that she was still upset about her house catching fire. I would be upset too.

"Are you feeling alright?" Grandma asked.

"We're not the same, Grandma," I lamented, as I sat down next to her on the sofa.

I was surprised that she nodded her head in agreement and replied, "This I know."

"I'm sorry for not telling you the truth about college."

"And I'm sorry for hitting you. You didn't deserve that."

"The fire was all my fault."

"It was not your fault. Don't you go blaming yourself."

"I just want you and Mama to be okay."

Grandma's eyes watered with tears as she placed her sewing items aside and turned off the TV with the remote.

"You know, I feared this day would come, but it came so fast. Seems like I blinked and the little girl in front of me was suddenly a woman."

"I just want you to be happy for me."

"Sweetheart, I am more than happy for you. You made me proud the minute you walked across that stage to get your diploma. I never wanted to hold you back from getting your education, but it was hard for me to let you go because..."

"Because what?"

Her lips quivered. "I was afraid something bad would happen to you like it did with your mother."

"I'm going to be just fine." I rested my hand on top of hers.

"I know it, but it won't stop me from worrying about you. New York is a mighty big city, child. Are you sure you're ready for all of that?"

"I'm ready because you prepared me so well."

"Aw honey, God bless you." She kissed my cheek.

"I love you, Grandma."

"And I love you too, more than you'll ever know."

CHAPTER 33
FAMILY IS A RELATIONSHIP

LUCCI

July 15, 1990

Yo, what's up Cousins!

I'm just getting your letters because we weren't allowed to have outside contact during the first few weeks of bootcamp, except for emergencies, but man I was so happy to receive letters from you guys. I was feeling terribly homesick out here in Ohio. All I can see from my window is green pastures. Last night, my bunkmates had to tell me that loud ongoing chirping sound outside was crickets. There is no civilization near us. Our building is in the boonies (as we say in DC). The only way for us to see other people is when the bus takes us into the city to clean the streets once a week. Cleaning the streets is part of our required community service. All the physical labor whipped a young buck like me into shape (check out the pictures of me flexing my muscles, but don't joan on my bald head. I know it's shaped like a peanut).

Can one of y'all do me a favor though? Holler at one of my homies, Kevin or Beanz up the block from Grandma's house and tell them to send me the latest Go-Go tapes. They are always at Eastside, so I know they got a Rare Essence or Northeast Groovers tape. And tell my old classmate Trina, once my hair grows back, I'll need her to shape it up for me since she's working at Lee's Barbershop on East Capitol Street now (per her letter). Ling and

Keisha wrote to me, and they're both preggers. I know I did too much synchronized swimming when I was living with them, but I'm going to be a good father when I get out.

Congratulations to Leslie for graduating from Eastern and earning a scholarship to Columbia. I'm so proud of you, big Sis! Your letter had me crying like Celie in The Color Purple. *How is my homey Mitch doing? I'm glad he took you to the prom. Tell him to write to me when he goes into the Navy.*

Boogie, congrats on making the cut to perform on "Showtime at the Apollo." Tell your mom to record it for me. It airs late out here in Ohio, and we have to be in bed by 9.

Yes guys, I heard about Turk getting life in prison. Guess who told me? My father! He wrote to me and said they shipped Turk to the same prison in Texas. Also, my dad sent me an article about my mom. She was sentenced to twenty years at a woman's prison in West Virginia. The feds found her in Miami. When she couldn't explain where she got the $20k that Turk gave her, they connected it to his enterprise. In the words of Grandma, "Glory to God, won't He do it?" Speaking of Grams, I'm sorry to hear about her house, but I'm glad ya'll were safely rescued. At least you can stay with Aunt Naomi while it's repaired.

Raven, nice picture of you and Adrian as King and Queen at his prom. You got my bunkmates drooling over you. Don't trip that Adrian got with another girl. Truth be told, I think you need to focus more on school anyway. Leave them sucker pretty boys alone before you get knocked up.

Well, I need to run. It's time for chow. I'm so thankful to y'all for loving me without an asterisk mark. Give the rest of the family my love!

Peace n' hair grease!
– Donovan "Lucci" Walker, Jr.

196

CHAPTER 34
THIS IS FOR LESLIE

MITCH

"I think that's enough balloons," I said to Raven. We were decorating Aunt Naomi's backyard for Leslie's surprise graduation-slash-going-away cookout party.

"A few more balloons won't hurt."

"It's a party for a teenager, not a little kid," I reminded her.

"Mitch is right, that's enough," Boogie agreed. "Besides, I'm tired of blowing balloons."

"Me too, I'm out of air," said his friend Nicole. She was a young cutie that Boogie invited to the party, along with his Rhythm Rock Boys dance crew. I wasn't sure which way was up with Boogie, but maybe one day he will figure it out for himself.

"Fine," Raven walked away and handled another task. She took the liberty of dumping more Little Hug juices in the coolers and covered them with ice.

I approached her. "Why do you always act like a brat?"

"I'm not a brat. I just don't like to be bossed around."

"Who is bossing you? I was simply stating my opinion."

She clucked her teeth and rolled her eyes.

"You need to grow up."

"I am grown." She propped one hand on her hip and fluffed her long hair with the other.

"Being grown is not about looks. That's why Adrian dumped you. You're too shallow."

"He didn't dump me. You can't break up with someone you're not in a relationship with."

197

"Well, he was smart enough to finally stand up for himself and move on."

"You're the one who instigated him to cut me off."

"I told him to have some spine, but it was his decision."

Raven tightened her lips and walked inside the house, upset. She was mad, but I didn't care. Adrian was a cool dude, but Raven treated him like crap. She was always bossing him around and he jumped at her beck and call. I was glad he was with Zoey. From our double dating, she respected him more than Raven ever did.

I helped Uncle Henry to fire up the grill. He gave me pointers on cooking ribs, burgers, and hotdogs. Aunt Naomi had Leslie preoccupied at Union Station with a shopping trip that included B. Dalton. I knew firsthand that Leslie could stay in a bookstore all day long, so we had plenty of time to get things ready for the party.

An hour later, guests started to arrive.

"Where should we put the gifts?" my mom, who came with Bernard, asked. I pointed to a round table that KC decorated with Leslie's name and the words, "Class of 1990."

Boogie plugged in his turntable and speakers to an extension cord that stretched from the house to out back. He started playing music as guests socialized, danced, and started to eat some of the finger food prepared.

Raven came rushing through the back door and approached me as I stood by the grill.

"Aunt Naomi just called. She and Leslie are on their way back from Union Station."

"I appreciate the heads-up. I'll quiet everyone down."

"Mitch, wait." Raven grabbed my hand. "I'm sorry for being a jerk. I'm going through a lot of different family changes right now."

"Don't I know it? This whole family has been through a lot. I'm just trying to help wherever I can, while I can."

"Thanks, Mitch. By the way, how is Adrian doing?"

"He's happy."

"Oh," her cheeks drooped.

"That doesn't mean *you* don't deserve to be."

She twiddled her thumbs. "You know, I didn't realize I was that bad."

"You'll be fine once you work through your family stuff."

"Really?"

I shrugged. "One can only hope, right?"

"Forget you, Mitch!" she hit me playfully.

We both shared a laugh.

CHAPTER 35
CONGRATULATIONS!

LESLIE

"SURPRIIIISE!"

My family and friends shouted as they blew confetti from their handheld cannons. They were all in the backyard of Aunt Naomi's house. I was wondering why there were so many cars out front.

"Oh, my goodness!" I yelped, covering my mouth in shock. Everyone hugged me and wished me well. I couldn't stop smiling. I never had a party like this before in my life.

A big "Congratulations" sign hung across the fence, along with baby blue and white party streamers and balloons that matched my school colors. The smell of charcoal and delicious barbeque filled the air while Boogie spun a new record, my favorite, Tony Toni Tone "Blues." Someone brought a bushel of steamed crabs from the Wharf and placed them on the picnic tables. We started chowing down. It felt so nice to celebrate with family and friends. As the evening wound down, different ones asked where I was going to college and what I was majoring in. They were so proud.

"You did it!" Aunt Diane hugged me.

"I was waiting for a 'but' followed by one of your infamous criticisms."

"Not this time," Aunt Diane stated as she took a deep breath. "Listen, I regret a lot of what I've done in life, especially with your mom, but I always wanted what was best for you. I'm so proud of you Leslie. Your mom would've been too."

"Thank you, Aunt Diane."

"I need everyone's attention!" Uncle Henry shouted as he walked over and rested his arm across my shoulder. We stood in the middle of the yard, and Boogie lowered the music as his dad began to speak.

"We are so happy for Leslie," Uncle Henry began. "She has set a fine example for the younger generation in this family. She was always looking after her cousins, her mom, and grandma. She never once complained. We wish her nothing but success at Columbia. Cheers to Leslie!"

"Yay! Congratulations Leslie!" everyone shouted. "Speech, speech, speech."

"Thank you everyone for coming out. I'm not used to all this attention. It feels awkward for me." My cheeks blushed bashfully. "You guys have meant everything to me. I wasn't sure I was ready to go away to college. I love my family so much, but now I realize that no matter where I go, I will carry you all with me in my heart."

"And Mitch too!" Raven shouted, and everyone laughed, including Mitch.

"Yes, and Mitch too," I giggled. "But seriously guys, I love you all, and thanks for supporting me."

Grandma stepped forward. "We love you too. Go and make us proud."

"To the class of 1990, congratulations to us!" KC and Devante shouted.

"This party is not over yet!" Boogie announced over the microphone. As soon as I heard the horns mixed with a conga drumbeat, I knew it was "Bustin Loose" by Chuck Brown. We all started dancing.

We formed the Soul Train line, and each person went down the aisle performing their best dance routine. I thought about the sleepover we had at Aunt Diane's house when we were kids. I saw Champ in my mind competing with Boogie, and Boogie out-dancing him. I saw Lucci dancing despite what he had just gone through at home, and I saw Raven trying to look cute. She never had any rhythm, even now as she danced down the aisle offbeat.

When it was my turn. I rocked my hips and arms to the beat, snapped my fingers, and danced like nobody was watching me. I realize that where you come from will always be your starting place in the world, and I will carry those lessons and memories with me forever. The time I've spent with my family, and especially my cousins, is a gift. Losing Champ taught me to cherish each day because tomorrow is not promised. Today, all we got is us!

ACKNOWLEDGEMENT

One of the first things I learned about writing was to write what you know and feel most passionate about. One of the closest subjects to my heart besides God is family. This book would not have been possible without them.

Many thanks to my husband for his input on this book project. To my son who patiently waited for my attention while I finished. Thanks to my mom who is my biggest supporter. She encourages me every day. Thanks to my siblings, nieces, nephews, and of course, my cousins. If not for the experiences we had growing up on Capitol Hill in Washington, DC, I wouldn't be who I am today.

I'm truly grateful to my phenomenal editor, Emily Michel, whose fine-tuning and gentle pen helped to shape this story. Emily, you rock!

Thank you to my beta readers who gave me the green light. I started on this story almost three years ago, and it's finally here.

Thank you to Karen Perkins at Lionheart Publishing, who always sacrifices herself to help her literary friends.

Last but certainly not least, thank you to my readers and supporters. Please remember to leave a review and spread the word about my books.

Cousins 2- Family Over Everything (F.O.E)
Coming Soon!

www.ingramcontent.com/pod-product-compliance
Lightning Source LLC
Chambersburg PA
CBHW071221290326
41931CB00037B/1771